CLARENCE H. ERICKSON

JESUS, THE HEALER DIVINE

Jesus, the Healer Divine

by

CLARENCE H. ERICKSON
Evangelist

(With Portrait)

Fifteen Sermons and Addresses to Seekers
for Scriptural Healing

(Third Edition)

"Himself took our infirmities and bare our sicknesses."
—Matt. 8:17

Published by the Author
REV. C. H. ERICKSON
P. O. Box 1302
INDIANAPOLIS, IND.

TABLE OF CONTENTS

PREFACE

The fact that a truth has been neglected does not invalidate it. Healing through the atoning power of Jesus Christ has attracted the sneers of the skeptic and the covert or open attacks of the nominal religionist until many good people have been fearful of accepting or practicing it. But through all ages the fact has remained—our living and mighty Lord heals those who come to him confiding in His will and believing in His Word.

The reader of these pages will find no attempt at literary style or the ornate use of language. Our object is to present the Gospel of healing in such simple terms and in the light of such plain Scriptural teaching that our readers will be at once led to a clear understanding of their privileges in Christ. In order to accomplish this result many passages of Scripture have been used repeatedly and commented upon from several angles.

The addresses which follow were all taken down stenographically just as they fell from the lips of the writer. This will account for considerable repetition and for errors in diction and language. We send this book forth, not as a model of English or composition but rather as a firebrand for the purpose of kindling renewed faith in Him who is the same "Yesterday, today and forever." And for any good that may be accomplished either for the souls or bodies of our readers we will ascribe all glory and praise unto the

King who ever liveth to abundantly fulfill all of His
wonderful promises.

CLARENCE H. ERICKSON,

Indianapolis, Ind.
June 8, 1927.

I

ARE THE DAYS OF MIRACLES PAST?

JESUS, THE HEALER DIVINE

I

ARE THE DAYS OF MIRACLES PAST?

There was a time when I was afraid to devote any set service to the discussion of Christ's power to heal the body lest it would detract from the revival spirit of the meeting. But I have found that when we preach what is in the Word of God we can depend on God's spirit through the Word to convict men. When I am preaching on healing, I do it not only with the motive that people will get faith for healing, but I believe this truth convicts men of sin.

I know there is a certain amount of alarm in the minds of the people concerning this subject—this is natural—and I would justify it to a certain extent. There is a fear on the part of many of fanaticism and wild fire. The danger is that we may be so afraid of it that we will have no fire at all. Never be afraid of God's Word. I believe we can very clearly show out of the Word of God that we have a right to believe today that God will do for us whatever he did for others in times past.

The Greatest Miracle

Tonight, my subject will be in the form of a question, "Are the days of miracles past?" It seems that there is no other one thought that is causing more unbelief in regard to healing than this one, with perhaps

11

the one exception of the doubt that people have, "If it be Thy will." Those two I would claim as the outstanding hindrances to faith for healing by Christ Jesus.

Many people have a wrong idea about miracles. They think that they no longer can be expected today. First, let me say this, Salvation is the greatest miracle of all miracles, and if God can do that great and wonderful miracle of changing a man's heart and taking out sin, why could he not do a lesser miracle—the healing of the body?

A man came to me today where we were staying —he does not live here, he is a traveling man. He was here last night, and was very much under conviction. He said, "I am a backslider and I want God to save me, and I want you to pray for me." He began to tell me of a certain thing that was holding him from which he was unable to break away. I told him of the power of God to break every band and set men free. This is the greatest miracle for it is beyond human power. It takes a supernatural touch. No man can be saved without believing in a miracle. The Bible tells us that every man that comes to God for salvation must believe that Jesus Christ died and rose again, and there you have the most outstanding miracles of sacred history and every man who believes Jesus Christ for salvation must accept a miracle for it. And then, as we explain salvation, we can only do so when we recognize it as a miracle. One man took exception when I spoke of salvation as being a miracle. I said to him, "What is it?" He said "It is the forgiveness of sins." "Yes, what is it?" I said, "Is it not a new birth?"

Jesus spoke to Nicodemus and said "Ye must be born again." Nicodemus could not understand that because it was something beyond the realm of nature, and he asked the question, "How can a man be born when he is old?" It is a miracle to be born again. It is a miracle to have the stony heart taken out and a heart of flesh put in. It is a miracle to have regeneration —not reformation—but regeneration.

A Changeless Christ

The first verse I want to give in answer to the question, "Are the days of miracles past?" is found in Hebrews 13:8, "Jesus Christ the same yesterday, and today, and forever." Now then, If Jesus Christ has changed, he is no longer the same, is he? If Jesus Christ will not today perform miracles of healing like he did when he was here on earth, then he has changed, has he not? When anyone comes to me with the thought that the days of miracles are past, I have always asked another question, "When did the miracles stop and when did Jesus Christ stop doing the things he said he would do?" And I have not found anyone yet who could give me a correct answer. They could not say it was at the time of the apostles. It happened after the apostles were all gone. When Jesus Christ was here on earth he went around and healed all the sick people, without any exceptions, did he not? But you say he will not do that today. How do you know? How dare we limit God's power? First, friends, I have found some people who do not deny that Jesus **could** do it, but say he does not do it, that it is not his will to do it, that he has some other way to do it now, and that he only healed the sick in ancient times to show them that he could do it. However, that was not his motive at all. Jesus Christ never healed folks just to show the people that he could do it, nor yet to show men that he was the Divine Son of God. He did it because he was the Son of God. If it had been his desire just to show that he could do it, all that he would have needed to have healed would have been a few isolated cases. It would not have been necessary to heal everybody, would it?

There is one outstanding thing in the life of Jesus Christ that I want to dwell on for a moment in order to use it in connection with the text: "Jesus Christ the same yesterday, and today, and forever." We find that there was one underlying principle that prompted Jesus to heal the sick, and that was his compassion, his love, his heart that went out to humanity. The need of men was so great and his love was so great that his very nature caused him to supply that need. Jesus said to the disciples, "What shall I do for I have compassion on the multitude?" They wanted to send the people away, back to their homes in the city that they might find something to eat. Jesus said, "No, you feed them." Sometimes the disciples of Jesus Christ have been sending people away down to the city or somewhere else to find something that would feed their hearts when they ought to have taken them to Jesus. He is the same in his love as he ever was. When he was here on earth it was to reveal the will of God to men, and that will has never changed. He was then as though he was running for office. He was showing us what he would do, what he was willing to do, what he could do, and revealing his great compassion. Now he is in office. Would you have the Savior like some politicians that run for office? When they first go before the people they say that when they are in they are going to do this and that and the other thing—going to have farm relief, better roads, and a hundred and one other improvements or reforms. But when they get into office they forget all about their promises. Some people think of Christ in that way today. "Now he is in office in heaven, and I don't believe his power is limited and neither do I believe his love is limited, but in office he no longer does what he did when on earth. Now he has been elected and he is up on high and we can not trust him any longer." Friends, that is not so. When he was here on earth he had the people and their needs at heart. He was at all times interested in our common humanity, and now, friends, Jesus Christ is still interested in the people. He is on high making intercession for you and me. Read Hebrews 4:15, 16; "We have not an high priest which cannot be touched with the feeling of our infirmities; but was in all points tempted like as we are, yet without sin. Let us, therefore, come boldly unto the throne of grace, that we may obtain mercy, and find grace to help in time of need." I have known politicians who, when running for office, would go out on the farms and talk about the mule and the cows and the crops, and everything else, but after the election when they were at Washington, D.C., or at the State House, you never could get near them. You could shake hands with them before and they would shake hands with you, but afterwards you could not touch them. Some people think that now Jesus Christ is in office and you can no longer expect him to mingle with men any more. But I do not believe he has changed one iota. He is still willing to do all that you and I have need to be done.

Afraid of Scarecrows

There is another class of people who disbelieve because they are in a backslidden condition. Some of them know that they would have to confess their sins before they could in any way believe for the supernatural. Therefore they deny it all and excuse themselves. But there are some who are very conscientious —they are afraid of wild fire, and therefore stay away as far as they can, like the horse that shys at the automobile. The devil I know has his counterfeit, but the counterfeit only shows there is the genuine. We have counterfeit United States money, but we do not have counterfeit Confederate money. Why? Because there is no real Confederate money. You are willing to acknowledge that we have the counterfeit but the only reason we can get the counterfeit is because there is the real. Thousands are seeking out the counterfeit because they fail to see the real. The devil has his scarecrows and has his imitations. Mrs. Erickson and I drove from California to this meeting—we came through the Mohave Desert and the Salt Lake Desert. Sand and sage brush could be seen for miles. I never saw a scarecrow anywhere. I did not see any pair of pants and coat and hat and straw to keep the birds away from the cherry trees because there was nothing out there but sand and sage brush. If you see any scarecrows around on God's farm you can make up your mind there is something there for you to eat. Look beyond the scarecrows.

One day when I was a boy I planted some beans. I knew there were woodchucks around there. I stuffed up a man and put him out by the bean patch. One of the woodchucks saw it. He went up and looked at the figure closely, and then my beans all disappeared. And yet there are people who seem not to have the ability to discern spiritual things that a woodchuck has to find his food.

Once when we lived in a city we would take the street car just as far as it would go and then get off and walk into the country to find an apple orchard. I would not be willing to admit that we stole apples —we just appropriated them. It was necessary that we spend just as little time as possible in that orchard because if the farmer ever found us there you know what would have happened. We always knew what tree had the sweet apples. How do you suppose we knew? Some of you fellows know. We never hit the crab apple tree. We would look into the apple orchard for the tree that had tin cans and old shoes around it. That was the sweet apple tree. We always went to that tree.

A lot of people look at Divine Healing and see the scarecrow of doubt or fanaticism. They try to eat the paper off of the can and never get what is inside of the can. You are entitled to eat the paper on the can and eat old shoes if you wish to do so, but I prefer to look beyond that and see the real, and ask God to give it to me. You need not be afraid of God.

Christ's Word to Us

Some are conscientious. They really think that the days of miracles are all over. They think Christ only performed miracles to establish his ministry, and since then they are no longer necessary. They argue that it was only Jesus Christ and his disciples who healed the sick. We find Jesus Christ healed all the sick that were around about, then he gave power to the Twelve, and they healed all that were sick and afflicted. Then there was so much of a need along that line that they were not able to meet it, so Jesus sent out seventy others. They had power to cast out devils and heal the sick. They came home and said, "Even the devils are subject unto us in thy name." Then, lo and behold they came in and met the Master, and said, "We found some other people casting out devils in thy name." They wanted to stop them. Jesus said, "Let them alone." Evidently they were converts, believers; they had heard the Word and were practicing it. He never would have said what he did if they had been wrong, or the counterfeit. They were others—not of the twelve, or the seventy—others.

We find Jesus healed the people, we find the Twelve doing it, the seventy doing it, and then Jesus Christ's time arrives and he ascends on high, but before he went away he left us some definite things that we might claim. He said in the 14th chapter of John, the twelfth verse, "He that believeth on me, the works that I do shall he do also; and greater works than these shall he do; because I go unto my Father." That does not say that the miracles are done away. "In my name you will do it." "Whatever you will ask in my

name I will do it that the Father might be glorified."
He asked us to ask largely "that your joy might be
full." After his resurrection he said to his disciples
(and every commentary will agree that it was not
merely the disciples, Mark 16, but to all who will
believe), "Go ye into all the world." Now it could
not have meant only the twelve because it was impossible for the twelve to have gone into all the world
and to preach the gospel to every creature. I believe,
friends, that this city is a part of that world that
Jesus Christ had reference to here. He said "every
creature." That includes you and me. Then, he very
definitely tells us what to teach. "He that believeth
and is baptized shall be saved, but he that believeth
not shall be damned. And these signs shall follow
them that believe." That is, not the twelve disciples,
not the seventy—it merely said "these signs shall follow them that believe." In all the world, to every
creature everywhere—whether it be preacher or lay-
man. . . . These were Jesus Christ's own words before he ascended on high.

A Whole Gospel Wanted

I like a whole gospel for a whole man, not a half
gospel. Why should I preach just a part of the gospel?
Why not have the privilege of preaching it all? There
is power in the name of Jesus Christ. The seventy
came back and said even the devils are subject to us
in thy name. Jesus said, "whatever you ask in my
name I will do it." And here he says "these signs
shall follow them that believe, in my name they shall
cast out devils, they shall speak with new tongues,

they shall take up serpents; and if they drink any deadly thing, it shall not hurt them." And I believe we have a right to claim that. If I am a missionary of the gospel out where a deadly malarial fever or plague of some kind is raging, I have a right to claim protection for myself in the name of Jesus and to believe that God will take care of me as long as I am in His will. I have gone into many homes where there were contagious diseases. I went in the name of Jesus and prayed God to protect me, and he never failed me. "They shall lay their hands on the sick and they shall recover." How many of the sick will recover, do you suppose? Do you believe just a part of them? A small portion? Now and then, an occasional one? If that is so, how am I to be certain but that only a few of those who believe will be saved? Doctor Gordon, in his book on healing, gives this story. An infidel was arguing with a minister about the Bible. The infidel believed that the Bible was done away and was simply fiction. He had the floor first, and turned to the preacher and said, "I want to ask you one question and you are to answer." He read this portion of Scripture. He said, "Is this so, that we have a right to expect to lay our hands on the sick and they will recover?" Then he sat down. The preacher got up and began to explain it away. He said "that is so in this sense, that it used to be so. It was, in the early church, necessary for these things to take place to establish the church and that people might believe, but it is no longer necessary." He sat down, and the infidel stood up. He said "All right, you do away with the last half of that great commission and

I will do away with the first half. That used to be back yonder, but that is no longer so." He sat down and there was no more to be said.

"After the Lord had spoken unto them he was received up into heaven and they went forth and preached everywhere, the Lord working with them, and confirming the Word with signs following. Amen." That means let it be so. That great commission is for you and me. We practice the first part, why should we neglect the last part? One old Scotchman said "What God has joined together let no man put asunder." I do not believe that a part of it has been done away. Some consider that it is like a dinner menu in a restaurant at three o'clock in the afternoon. You sit down and say, "I believe I will have tenderloin steak." The waiter says, "I am sorry, it is all gone." You see there is some roast beef on the menu. You order it. The waiter replies, "I am sorry, we are all out of that." You say, "I will have to take something left over—some liver or bacon or hash." So some would say that the apostles got all the good and all we have is a little that is left.

God's Miracles Continue Today

The days of God's miracles are not over but they are continuing today. After Jesus Christ ascended and we are ushered out of the gospels, we are taken into the life of the apostles and the ministry of the church. After He arose from the grave he did as he said he would do. He said he was going away but would send another Comforter. What we read in the Acts is not the Acts of the apostles, but the Acts of the Holy Ghost through the apostles and church of Jesus Christ in that time. I believe we are living in the dispensation of the Holy Spirit, and He is continuing to do what Jesus Christ began to do and to teach. And all the way through the Book of the Acts you find mention of healing. Philip was not a disciple, not an apostle. Stephen was not an apostle. He was a man filled with the Holy Ghost, and the people believed him and came and sought what he had. Simon the sorcerer wanted to buy the power and wanted to do what Philip was doing. The signs and wonders were following. Things were taking place. He was merely a man who was filled with the Holy Ghost, and an elder in the church.

We have the Holy Spirit today and I believe He wants to work in this body, and in the church. We are the body of Jesus Christ. We belong to God's church here. We have local organizations—Methodists, Baptists, Presbyterians—but only one body of Jesus Christ, and you and I have been born into one body and Jesus Christ is the head of that body, the church. The same Holy Spirit is working out in the body of Jesus Christ, or the church, today. The church should have in it that same miracle-working power that Jesus manifested because He is the head of the church. I can find no place in the Bible that would cause me to believe that the days of miracles are over or that God does not answer prayer today, that he does not heal.

If I did not believe that I would not preach the gospel at all. If I did not believe that we have a living God I would not be in the ministry at all. If

I could not preach the whole Bible as it is I would not preach any of it. If one part of it is faulty, then all of it is very suspicious to me. If I can not believe it like it is and accept it and get down on my knees and reach out by faith and say "God make it real," I would not want to be in the ministry. I am in it because I believe God's word with all my heart. It has worked in my life. God has taken care of me when it seemed nothing could help me. God has supplied needs when man never knew it. I was just reading the life of George Mueller who prayed in seven million dollars. He wanted to show to the world that we have a real God who answers prayer. God is real! Never be discouraged. Numbers of Christian people have prayed for something and did not get it. Very soon their prayers become routine, they fail to expect that for which they ask, and would be surprised if they did receive it. Let us show to the world that we have a God who does answer prayer. You say "I am sick in body." You have a right to be healed. You have a right to expect God will do it for you. He is no respecter of persons.

II

A WHOLE GOSPEL—SALVATION FOR THE SOUL
AND HEALING FOR THE BODY

A WHOLE GOSPEL—SALVATION FOR THE SOUL AND HEALING FOR THE BODY

"When Jesus saw him lie, and knew that he had been now a long time in that case, he saith unto him, Wilt thou be made whole? The impotent man answered him, Sir, I have no man, when the water is troubled, to put me into the pool: but while I am coming, another steppeth down before me. Jesus saith unto him, Rise, take up thy bed, and walk. And immediately the man was made whole, and took up his bed, and walked: and on the same day was the sabbath. The Jews therefore said unto him that was cured, It is the sabbath day: it is not lawful for thee to carry thy bed. He answered them, He that made me whole, the same said unto me, Take up thy bed, and walk. Then asked they him, What man is that which said unto thee, Take up thy bed, and walk? And he that was healed wist not who it was: for Jesus had conveyed himself away, a multitude being in that place. Afterward Jesus findeth him in the temple, and said unto him, Behold, thou art made whole: sin no more, lest a worse thing come unto thee."—Jno. 5:6-15.

I want you to look with me into this lesson on healing. Jesus came to the Pool of Bethesda, and a man was there who had been afflicted for thirty-eight years. The angel came down and troubled the waters, whether regularly or occasionally we do not know, but at certain seasons the water was troubled and whoever got into the water first was made whole. It was only one who was healed, and that, the first one. Jesus came to this man who had been afflicted for thirty-eight years. Peculiarly, and just in passing, I would say that it was strange but it seems to have been a deliberate act, this healing on the sabbath day. Jesus seems to have done it that he might show to the people of all time that it was a spiritual blessing and one we can receive on a holy day as well as any other day.

A Striking Question

Now Jesus, as he came to the man asked him a very striking question. It seems foolish when you first think of it, but as you know Jesus Christ would do no foolishness for in the life of Christ there was no joking or joshing. He came up to the man who had been waiting for thirty-eight years, and said, "Wilt thou be made whole?" Had he wanted to be like many today he would have replied, "Such a foolish question to ask a man. Here I am sick for thirty-eight years, and then you ask me, Do I want to get well. Such a strange question." Nevertheless, that question brings out a great truth. There must be a will in the matter of wanting to be well. First we must find out His will, and then we must set our will in harmony with God's will to get the blessing, then we will get it. The Bible tells us in I Timothy 6:12 "Lay hold of eternal life." **Lay hold of it!** That does not mean to sit idly by and say, If God wants to give it to me all right and if not all right.

We have some people who mistake laziness in faith for the rest of faith. It is a lack of faith not to go out and test God's promises. When the Word tells us to receive the Holy Ghost, that Word means to exercise faith that he may come in to abide. People say, well if God wants to give me the Holy Ghost I will not object, I will take him. No man ever received the Holy Ghost that way. If he got the blessing it was when he sought for it and made up his mind to have it, and believed for it, and so received it. No man sits back in his seat and says, If God wants to I will let him, and gets it.

Jesus asked a question that was very logical. He said, "Wilt thou be made whole?" When we put our wills in God's will and determine to get the answer, then we will get healing. I have seen people come in a passive state of mind for healing. One man said "I am a little bit deaf. It don't bother me much. If I would not get healed it won't make much difference." He never got it! When you come in that frame of mind you get nothing. There must be a will to receive before we will have the faith to receive. Put your will with God's will. Simply say that God has provided for it and, by God's grace I will have it. It is a very fair question—"Wilt thou be made whole?"

The Man's Answer

The man answered him this way. He said "I have no man to put me in the water." First, he was looking to someone else to hand the blessing to him. Some people say, "I had so and so pray for me, but I did not get anything so I thought I would try you." Get your eyes off of man and on to God. No man can heal you, it is God that heals you. In one place we had so many to pray for I got tired and I asked somebody else to pray. Some would take their cards and go home. Nor could they get anything when they came to me. You obey God in being anointed and prayed for, and get the blessing. Look to God as you obey his Word.

Then, again, there is another thought implied, that is, that he was just putting off his healing into the future. He thought some time somebody would push him into the pool. If you are going to receive healing you must put a time limit on it. You cannot say any time, anywhere, any place, but, "Lord, I believe you, heal me now," not any time. The eleventh chapter of Mark tells us "What things soever ye desire when ye pray, believe that ye receive them, and ye shall have them." Not just a hope that some day you will get the blessing. We want you to get your eyes on Jesus and be determined to get it and get it now.

Jesus and the Use of Means

One thought there is here I might just use in passing. Jesus did not have an angel come down and trouble the waters and then place the sick man in the pool. No. You might think the water had healing power. Some people think you must use means. Jesus did not use any natural remedy or natural means. He did not even trouble the water; he just said to the man, "Arise, take up thy bed, and walk." I suppose the man might have asked the question as some would ask today—"How can I walk? I have been here thirty-eight years." At first the man did not know to whom he was talking. Jesus said, "Arise." The sick man might have said, "If I could have arisen and gone about by myself why would I be lying here all this time?" I prayed for some people on this platform who did about like that. I prayed for a lady who was deaf. I said "Say, praise the Lord." The other lady who was with her said, "She cannot hear out of that ear." She did not expect it at all.

Making the Start

Some want to argue with the Lord instead of doing what he says to do and doing it right away. You will miss the blessing many times by not obeying quickly what God tells you to do. It is your business to try and to put forth an earnest effort to have it, and it is God's business to fulfill His promises. Just as soon as the man made the start God put new energy and vitality into him so that he was able to stand. Then he picked up his bed and afterwards went into the temple. Somebody saw him carrying his bed on the sabbath. Who told you to do this?" He answered, "He that made me whole." He did not know who it was. Later when he was in the temple Christ saw him and said, "Sin no more, lest a worse thing come unto thee." And the Word tells us that straightway he knew that it was Jesus who had healed him.

"Sin no More"

Any healing Jesus has anything to do with is coupled up with "sin no more lest a worse thing come upon you." These truths go side by side. Preach the gospel and heal the sick. Jesus said, "Thy sins are forgiven thee, thou art healed of thy plague." He said, "Arise, sin no more." I find that from Calvary two streams are flowing—the one for the healing of our body and the other for the healing of our soul. They run parallel. Where you find one you ought to find the other all the time. I do not believe they should be separated. Some people want to take one stream and not the other. Some say, I will take the stream for sin and leave the other stream. Some people take one stream, the stream of healing, and separate it away from the other, "sin no more." They want bodily healing without the forgiveness of sin. But if you are coming for healing and

your body is afflicted, I say unto you also, sin no more
lest a worse thing come upon you.

— Friends, how beautiful is the plan of salvation;
how wonderfully it has been arranged. The two run
together all the time. We cannot separate them.
Back yonder they did not doubt that Jesus Christ
could heal the body, but when it came to forgiveness
of sin, they said, "who is this blasphemer, that says
he can forgive sin?" Today we say Christ can forgive
sins, but that He cannot heal the body any longer. I
say as the Scotchman that Doctor Gordon writes about
in his book, "What God hath joined together let no
man put asunder." A sin-destroying religion and a
perfectly well body, both of them in the name of Jesus
Christ! Hallelujah!

I am glad for this gospel tonight. I feel just as
much at home in this tabernacle as I would in my
own house because I believe in a gospel that is practical
and I know it works. If you are sick in body, come
and let Jesus Christ heal that body and you will have
every reason to rejoice. If there is sin in your heart,
thank God he can take away sin and cleanse your heart
and make you whole. I am glad for a full gospel tonight, one that takes in not only a part of a man but
a whole man. I am glad I am serving Jesus who can
do this for us, as men and women have been seeing,
as they saw that little girl, unable to walk; the little
baby born blind, now beginning to see. This is not
man's work—it is God's work. When you are coming
in contact with that you are coming in contact with the
supernatural. This is God's revival.

III

GOD'S WILL REGARDING OUR HEALING

GOD'S WILL REGARDING OUR HEALING

Many when coming for prayer for the body are well aware that God is able to heal the body. That is perhaps one of the commonest sayings when persons are coming—they say "I know God is able." But, friends, faith must rest on something besides knowing He is just able to do it. We must be able to overcome that common phrase that is used so many times: "If it be Thy will."

Jesus is Easy to Approach

Here are several instances of healing in the ministry of Jesus Christ. The first one uses that very phrase in just a little different wording. It is in the 8th chapter of Matthew, "And behold, there came a leper and worshipped him, saying, Lord, if thou wilt, thou canst make me clean." That is just the same as "Lord I know you are able, but is it your will?" He says "if thou wilt, thou canst make me whole." This leper knew that Jesus Christ could do it. He did not reason and say, "I know leprosy is hard and it is the worst case and I do not know whether he could do it or not." Somewhere he had learned that Jesus Christ was equal to anything. So he came to Jesus Christ—came right where he was. And that is one thing I like about Jesus Christ in his earthly ministry—he was willing for anyone to come to him from anywhere and in any way. He did not hold himself aloof from the people. When I was in the army we had one Major, and he was a Major and he knew it. He was so big and all-important that nobody could reach him at all. He would not allow a Private to stay at headquarters when he was there. Jesus Christ, even though Divine, let anyone come to him.

Jesus and "If"

This leper said "If thou wilt thou canst make me whole." Notice the answer Jesus gave him, "And Jesus put forth his hand, and touched him, saying, I will; be thou clean." No ifs about it. He would immediately take away the "if" when it comes to his will.

Another man mentioned in the Bible came to him, he said, "Lord, if thou canst do anything, have mercy." Jesus immediately turned around, and said "If thou canst believe." When the man came to him and realized his power to do it, but did not know whether he would do it, he said "if thou wilt." Jesus takes the "if" right away. Many folks say "If it is thy will I know you can." Jesus takes away that "if."

There is no faith whatever in just knowing that God can do it. There must be a revealing of the will of God before there is faith. I will illustrate that. I have half a dollar in my hand. That is mine. I can do anything with it that I wish. I can give it to Brother L. here if I desire to do so. Do you think you are going to get it, Brother L.? I can give it to him if I wish but instead I put it in my pocket. He knows I can do it, but that does not produce faith. A bank can loan me $100 but that is no sign it will make such a loan. You might get it but I do not think they are willing to give it to me. Our faith stands upon knowing that God will do it.

Christ's Willingness to Heal

I want to read a good number of verses here. I want you to notice the one outstanding thought in all of them, the willingness of Jesus Christ to heal. He never turned anyone away. And in connection with this thought tonight, and as I read about the willingness of Christ to heal, just read this verse: "Jesus Christ is the same yesterday, today," and, as one brother had a man writing it, he said "tomorrow." In every way he was, he is the same today. If a leper comes to him tonight and says "If thou wilt thou canst make me whole," Jesus would say the same as before, "I will." If he would not, he would be a respecter of persons, and we know he is not a respecter of persons. Jesus said, "I will. Be thou clean." Immediately his leprosy was cleansed. And Jesus saith unto him, "See thou tell no man; but go thy way, shew thyself to the priest, and offer the gift that Moses commanded, for a testimony unto them."

We will go right on to another. "And when Jesus was entered into Capernaum, there came unto him a centurion beseeching him, and saying, Lord, my servant lieth at home sick of the palsy, grievously tormented. And Jesus saith unto him. I will come and heal him." One lady from Ohio wrote to Brother K. who was here for a while. He advised that she write to me. She wrote me a very long letter. She said, "I have cancer of the stomach and doctors have given me up. I am a mother of three children. They are very young and I don't want to die. Not that I am not ready to, but I want to live that my children will have a mother for a few more years. I have written Brother K. and he asked me to write to you. I want you to fast all day and pray for me, and find out if it is God's will to heal me. Then write me frankly, and if you believe it is not God's will to heal me, tell me.'' I wrote her a letter. I did not fast all day and did not pray all day. I already knew. I wrote her several long pages. I said it was not necessary for me to pray all day and fast, because I had the Bible and could read it and find out his will right here. I believe in finding out the will of God in his Word. I am not prone to find out the will of God by visions or special revelations. One man came to me with his peculiar doctrine and tried to explain it to me. I said ''I can't see it at all.'' He said ''You will have to get it by special revelation.'' I said ''I don't want it, then.'' The Bible says that the way is so plain that a fool does not need to err therein. I said to this seeker, ''It is fine that you want to be well and take care of your children, but the argument for you to use is that he has promised it to you even if you had no children. It does not say if a mother has six children she will be healed. It says ''If there is any sick among you.'' There are no qualifications. It is his will. The leper said ''If it is thy will.'' Jesus said, ''I will.'' The centurion said ''My servant is home sick.'' He said, ''I will come and heal him.'' The centurion answered and said, ''I am not worthy.'' You never could merit God's blessings. They are free gifts. You do not merit them, you do not work for them, you receive them as a free gift.

Healing Through No Merit of Ours

You will not be healed because of your own merits. Someone asked me who is it who receives the most healing, is it always the best people or the sinners who come in and get it. This question bothered me for a while. I began to study and to watch. Many people have their good works right in front of them and they believe they will get healed because of good works. Come for healing to receive it through Jesus Christ and his merit alone. Never come feeling worthy in yourself. The centurion said "I am not worthy that thou shouldst come under my roof, but speak the word only and my servant shall be healed. For I am a man under authority, having soldiers under me: and I say to this man, Go, and he goeth; and to another, Come, and he cometh; and to my servant, Do this, and he doeth. When Jesus heard it, he marvelled, and said to them that followed, Verily I say unto you, I have not found so great faith, no, not in Israel."

Jesus said, "I have not found so great faith, no, not in Israel. The centurion said, "You don't have to come," but Jesus said "I will come." And then, just going over to the 13th verse, we follow it up. "And Jesus said unto the centurion, Go thy way; and as thou hast believed, so be it done unto thee." Note the past tense he uses there, "As thou hast believed." He did not say "As you are going to believe."

So many people believe that God is going to do it; that it is going to be done sometime, when, how or where they do not know, but sometime, any time, anywhere. This centurion believed and Jesus said "As thou hast believed, so be it done unto thee. And his servant was healed in the self same hour.''

"And when Jesus was come into Peter's house, he
saw his wife's mother laid, and sick of a fever. And
he touched her hand, and the fever left her: and she
arose, and ministered unto them.'' There are four cases
of healing right there in the first few verses. In the
next two or three verses, whole multitudes are healed.
Why? The will of Jesus Christ was to heal all who
came to him in faith believing. "When the even was
come, they brought unto him many that were possessed
with devils: and he cast out the spirits with his word,
and healed.'' **Part** of those who were sick? **Some**
of them? **Almost** all of them? No, he healed all—all
that were sick that were brought unto him. We have
a Christ who is the same today as he was then, and
he will heal all who will come just the same today as
he did then. Not part of them, not if we are lucky,
but all of us.

He Heals All

One says, "I know he heals some people but, of
course, he does not heal everybody.'' How are we
going to know who he will heal? If he will heal you
and not me, he thinks more of you than of me. Maybe I have money and you have not. Any person has
a right to come and expect the same tender Christ to
do for him as he will do for anyone else. He healed
all who were brought to him. Why? Just to show
the people that he could do it? Just to strut all around
revealing his deity and showing his great power and
majesty? No. Matthew tells us in the 17th verse of
this chapter that "He healed all that were sick that it
might be fulfilled which was spoken by Esaias, the

prophet, saying, Himself took our infirmities and bare our sicknesses." He must heal them all because he said he bore our diseases and took our sins. Was it a part of our sins, a few of us, that he bore the sin for a few and not for all? That "**our**" takes in you and me and everybody else. It is "whosoever will," not just a part of us.

Once I was very earnestly seeking for a deeper spiritual life, and I was very much wrought up about it, and I wanted so much to know the Lord better. I would see people go to the altar. They had a big inquiry room there. I would watch them. I would see some man go into a certain corner and he would get wonderfully blessed of the Lord. I would hear the shouts. The next night when the altar call came I would kneel in the same place. I would think, "It will hit me here tonight." But it never hit me there at all; it was always missing me. Some seekers try healing just like that. They see someone get it here and they run over and imagine it will hit them in the same place. But God doesn't do business that way. He will do for you whatever he will do for anybody else, and you need not sit in the same seat or go in the same line or look to one certain evangelist. If you come and believe God, you can come with just this much assurance that he will do for you what he does for anybody else.

I like the Word because he said he healed them all. You go through the New Testament and you will find he was healing them all, all, all, **ALL, ALL, ALL**— was always healing them **ALL.** He did not say, "You just stay sick for God's glory." He did not say, "I want you to be sick for a little while. You can glorify

me a little better." No, no. They were sick. Jesus
Christ was healing them all, all the time. Is there a
reason why I should come and question God's will?
Should we come to the Lord and say I know you can
do it, I know you have the power to do it, now if you
will do it. You know, friends, I can often tell when
people come to be prayed for whether they have faith
or not. One lady in particular came, and was being
anointed and prayed over, and she just threw her hands
up and began to cry and beg. She said, "Lord, you
said you would do it; I know you are able to do it.
Now, Lord, please do it, if it is thy holy precious will."
I had to quit praying. I looked at her and said
calmly, "I wish you would come back a little later. I
would like to talk to you because you haven't got
faith." She said, "Yes, I have all kinds of faith." I
said, "That is it, it is all kinds and not the right kind."
She said, "I have been a Christian a long time." I
said, "I am glad to know that, but," I said, "you don't
know whether God is going to do this or not." "I
know he can do it," she said. "But sister," I said,
"faith does not rest upon knowing God can do it. It
rests upon the revealed will of God." That is the reason
for our question on the card, "Are you convinced
that it is God's will to heal you?" If not, the first
thing to do is to find out whether it is God's will or
not. Just read it and find he never turned anyone
away and he has promised to do it. If I believe, he is
able and he said he would do it. Do I have to say
then, "I know you have promised to do it, I know you
can do it if you will do it. I am needing it now." No,
I will not come that way, nor did I come that way. If

I see God said he would do it I know he has the power to do it and has promised to do it, and I look up and say, "thank you, Lord Jesus, I will just accept it and thank you in advance."

Believe God's Promise

If Brother L. told me at twelve o'clock he was going to give me a thousand dollars, do you suppose I would sit around and cry and look long-faced and go home and say, "Of course, Brother L. said he would give it to me but I don't have it yet?" If I believed he was going to do it I would go home and say, "I am going to get the car out and go after it." I would not go up to Brother L. tomorrow half crying and looking sad and cautious, and say "I know you said you would give me that one thousand dollars last night," and then wave my hands around him and say "I know you can do it, if you will, Brother L., I would like to have it." Do you suppose I would come like that? Instead I would drive over there and say, "thank you, I am over here to get that thousand dollars" and there would be no "if" about it. I would just take it. Come to God like that. Let us have as much confidence in God as we would have in each other. If I could believe Brother L., that he would give me that one thousand dollars, my wife and I would be sitting up all night thinking what we were going to do with it. We would find some place for it. We would plan. "The first thing, we will put it in the bank. We will pay so and so. We will pay that note, and do this and that. We would begin to spend it already." Many of you are spending the money already that you are going to get next payday. You work a whole week long and expect to get your pay at the window. You never whine and cry about it, when they have you on the payroll.

You are still seeking. It said, let the needy praise him. Let everything that hath breath praise the Lord. A sick man has breath, does he not? When he uses that little breath he will get more. You say "I am still sick." Then praise the Lord. "I haven't got anything to praise the Lord for." You praise him for what he is going to do. That is faith, that is honoring God. That is what we need today—men and women who will believe God and honor him by thanking him. "Let your requests be known with thanksgiving," not by teasing. Thank God in advance for the blessing. Why? Because he said so. That is enough.

IV

HEALING IN THE ATONEMENT

IV

HEALING IN THE ATONEMENT

In the 5th chapter of Romans the 12th verse we are told that sin entered into the world and death by sin, and inasmuch as sin is incipient death and sin brought death and sickness, there was no sickness or death until first there was sin. Sickness is the fruit of sin. It might be called the child of sin. And why anyone should want to coddle the fruit or child of sin is more than I know. Why can we not see it in its true light and earnestly desire to get rid of it?

Sickness Is Not a Blessing

Many people fail to find faith for healing for the simple reason that they look at sickness in the wrong light—they look on it as a blessing. Of course, if that is so they should not ask God to take away a blessing. If he has made us sick, of course, it is a blessing. Supposing the brother here has the lumbago. If he looks at it as a blessing he ought to ask God to give his wife some of it. He ought not to be stingy with it but want to share it! Suppose Brother L. has the rheumatism. He ought to praise the Lord for it and pray the Lord to give me a little of it and not to have it all for himself. Those who believe in the second blessing in the spirit ought to ask God to give them a second blessing in the body. If they have rheumatism they ought to ask God to give them lumbago along with it. Thus if you have a toothache you should not go down to the dentist and have him pull the blessing out. It is inconsistent, and our actions are often incon-

47

sistent with our belief. People say they believe their
sickness is a blessing, and instead of praising God for
that blessing, and that they are in the sweet will of
God, they go to the drug store and get some of Sloan's
liniment or something and try to get rid of it!

Sickness Is the Result of Sin

Sickness came into the world as a result of sin. I
do not mean that because you are sick you have
sinned, but sickness primarily came into the world as
a result of sin. You may come in contact with sickness and thereby get sick, but that sickness itself came
into the world as a result of sin. For anything that
came as a result of sin we must naturally go to Calvary
for its remedy. I want to take you back to Calvary as
a basis for healing. In the Old Testament we find the
types and shadows of things to come and of Christ.
We find the life of Christ typified in the atonement and
the sacrifices—they are all typical of what should take
place. The children of Israel going through the desert
were bitten by the snakes. God told Moses to raise up
a serpent, and everyone who should look at that serpent
would live. Why was it that Moses was told to tell
the people to look at that serpent which was the type
of Jesus Christ? Few but will agree with me that
there was a type of Jesus Christ who should be hung
on a cross and raised up after being crucified. If healing is not in the atonement why were they told to look
at the type of Christ for healing of the body? If they,
back yonder, could be healed by the thousands in looking at just the type of Christ, why could we not today

The Serpent decayed Eave the cause of sin, so Moses held up the serpent so they saw the very cause of sin so Christ on the cross removed the

be healed by looking at the antitype, Jesus Christ himself?

One man made this point, about looking at symptoms. One thing to notice is that the people were told to look at the serpent on the pole. Evidently the snakes could not bite them around the neck but around the ankles or on the legs, and they were told to look up at the type of Christ on the cross. You could not look up there and at your symptoms at the same time unless you stood on your head and that would be hard to do. What we want people to do is to look at Christ and not simply the symptoms.

Look to Jesus on Calvary

One lady in California was prayed for but did not seem to get any healing. She was struggling along trying to believe and exercise her faith; but one night when I was preaching on healing in the atonement and that Jesus Christ bore our sicknesses as well as our sins, she saw the light and walked out underneath it and was made well sitting in her seat. Oh that we could see our privileges, walk out from underneath our burdens and see that he bore them on the cross!

The Prophecy of Isaiah Fulfilled

I want to read the 16th verse of the 8th chapter of Matthew. "When the even was come, they brought unto him many that were possessed with devils: and he cast out the spirits with his word, and healed all that were sick." Did you ever look through the New Testament in the life of Christ and find out how many times it was said he healed all that were sick, healed all who had need of healing, "they brought many and he healed them all?" This is another one of the times he healed all. The seventeenth verse reads, "That it might be fulfilled which was spoken by Esaias the prophet, saying, Himself took our infirmities, and bare our sicknesses." That is the reason that he healed them all, because it was our sicknesses and he could make no exception to any of them, because if he made any exception to the case it would not be all of our sicknesses, it would be **some.**

He quotes here from Isaiah the 53d chapter. He said, "He healed them all that it might be fulfilled." And friends, he is still healing them all "that it might still be fulfilled which was spoken by Esaias the prophet, saying, Himself took our infirmities, and bare our sicknesses." He is in the business of healing "all." Not some, but "all."

I know people who believe in divine healing in a measure, that is when you talk to them about it they say, "Oh, yes, I believe in divine healing all right, but"—and then they start to tell you all they do not believe and when they are through you wonder if there is anything left that they do believe. When people tell me that, I could almost add "But you don't believe it." But when it comes to believing in healing in the atonement of Christ and that he vicariously bore our sicknesses as well as our sins, that is a little more than they want to take. Why? Because they cannot consistently believe that healing is in the atonement of Jesus Christ and say that healing is for some people and not for others, because if it is in the atonement, the atonement is for every one. And if we accept healing in the atonement we must agree that all have a right to come and be healed because the atonement was made for us all, not just for some of us. And if you hold the theory that some people are sick for God's glory it would be very difficult for you to believe healing is in the atonement because the atonement of Jesus Christ includes us all—he bore our sicknesses, and if that is the case he will not expect us to bear them ourselves. He is telling us that it was fulfilled that the prophet said.

All of us agree that the 53d chapter of Isaiah is the atonement chapter of prophecy. I believe I will read the whole chapter. I don't know anything better to say than the Bible says. If the Bible says it, it must be so, and then you cannot say it is just what you believe. No, it is what the Bible teaches.

"Who hath believed our report? and to whom is the arm of the Lord revealed? For he," who is he speaking about there? He is speaking about Jesus. "For he shall grow up before him as a tender plant, and as a root out of a dry ground: he hath no form nor comeliness; and when we shall see him, there is no beauty that we should desire him. He is despised and rejected of men; a man of sorrows, and acquainted with grief."

The two words that are translated sorrows and grief are translated in many places in the Bible as pains and sickness, and you will find any commentary will agree with that, and if you do not like to take man's commentary for it, in Matthew 8:17 Jesus Christ interpreted it himself. He said "He bare our sicknesses." So the thought of sorrows and grief should in reality be pains and sicknesses.

"And we hid as it were our faces from him; he was despised, and we esteemed him not. Surely." Here comes the verse now that Jesus quotes and the Scripture emphasizes it by putting a "surely" in front of it. "Surely, he hath borne." "Hath borne" is the same word in the original language that is in the last verse. "He bare the sin of many." And just the same as he bore our sins, the same word or language is used to tell us that he bore our sicknesses.

"Surely he hath borne our griefs, and carried our sorrows; yet we did esteem him stricken, smitten of God, and afflicted. But he was wounded for our transgressions, he was bruised for our iniquities: the chastisement of our peace was upon him; and with his stripes we are healed."

Now let me read the 10th verse. "Yet it pleased the Lord to bruise him; he hath put him to grief: when thou shalt make his soul an offering for sin, he shall see his seed, he shall prolong his days, and the pleasure of the Lord shall prosper in his hand." "Put him to grief," or put him to sickness; and, as Doctor Gordon in his book on the Ministry of Healing puts it, he hath made him sickness who knew no sickness as he made him sin who knew no sin. So I am sure, friends, that we have a basis for our believing that Jesus Christ on Calvary bore our sicknesses just as he bore our sins.

Christ Our Scapegoat

The natural argument is this, if he bore them why should we have to bear them any longer? The scape goat in the Old Testament was a type of Christ. They would take the goat after making the offerings, and they made offerings in the Old Testament for many things. When it came to healing, they made atonements, offerings, sacrifices for healing. Why were they compelled and asked to make them if it was not looking forward to the coming great sacrifice for the healing of the body? They had the sacrifices and would take a goat and the priest would lay his hand on it and that would transmit to the goat the sins of all the people of Israel, and then they would send the goat outside the camp, and he was to go without in the desert and bear the sins of the people away. And friends, Jesus Christ became our scape goat, and on him was laid our sins and the penalty of our sin. And he went without the camp and suffered and bore our sicknesses and sins. If he did that, I do not have to bear my sins any longer, do I?

Deliverance from Penalty

I have heard people say this: "My sickness came as a result of my sin and I suppose I will have to bear the penalty for that sin." No you do not. God wants to deliver you from the penalty of sin as well as the sin itself. God can take out the nail print— as the old saying goes we can pull the nails out but the nail hole will be in the post. God takes the nail hole and all out—he bears the sin and its penalty.

One man came to me with the saddest story. He told me that he had been out in sin and as a result of sin became very sick. He said "I have given my heart to the Lord, but I suppose I will have to continue in this way." I said "No you do not. God can deliver you from it." He said "I am glad to know it," and he believed it. We prayed for him and he was wonderfully healed.

"And with his stripes we are healed." We are looking forward to Calvary. Peter, in the 2d chapter of his first epistle and in the 24th verse, is looking back to Calvary. Isaiah looked forward to it and Peter looked back to it, and both of them tell us what happened at Calvary. One says "By his stripes we are healed," and the other looks back and said "By his stripes ye were healed." It took place yonder on Calvary. So tonight we have a right to look back to Calvary and say "By his stripes we were healed," back yonder. One woman saw this truth while the preacher was preaching. She looked up and put her hand up and said "Praise the Lord, by his stripes I were healed." If we could see that we were healed back on Calvary that Christ bore our sicknesses as well as our sins, oh hallelujah, how we would want to walk out and take our portion!

"Forget Not All His Benefits"

How many of us are living on half rations when we might receive all and have perfectly well bodies as well as healing for our souls. But we have forgotten the promises and the power of God. The Psalmist David said not to forget all His benefits, and what is His reference there? Is it to the benefits of Jesus Christ on the cross, who forgives sin and heals all. Thank God for that all, all, all. I cannot read anything but that all. If he cleanses us from all, how many are left? How many sins will he not forgive?

If he heals all, how many are left that he will not heal? All is all.

As I think about the cross of Calvary, and healing in the atonement, and God's promises, and that we can benefit by them today, it makes me want to shout and praise the Lord for what he has done for us, as I think how unworthy we were and how wonderful He is. We can come to men with a perfect Savior who can meet our every need. As Jesus Christ was here on earth he met every need of man regardless of what it was. If it was to quiet the storm-tossed sea, he met that need. If it was to raise the widow's son, he met that need. If it was to multiply the bread or multiply the wine, he met that need. If it was to cast out the devil, he did that. No matter what it was, Christ met every need—leprosy, blindness, palsy, and all. In Christ we have a full supply for every need.

1 Cor. 1:30; "But of him are ye in Christ Jesus, who of God is made unto us wisdom, and righteousness, and sanctification, and redemption." Praise God, all this is in Christ. He said he would supply all our needs according to his riches by Christ Jesus. So he supplies our needs in Christ; whatever our need is we can go to Christ for it and can have it supplied. He gives us a full gospel that can meet every need— spirit, soul and body. Jesus Christ went to the cross in spirit, soul, and body for our spirit, soul and body, and what the first Adam lost the second Adam came to bring back, and you and I can look for in the second Adam what the first Adam lost. He has come to seek and to save that which was lost.

Do Not Go on Half Rations

I was very weary today, very tired. I have been very busy. I had little time to prepare for the evening sermon. As I got to thinking about it a little while and meditating, the Lord made me so happy in the message, it seemed to make very little difference whether I could speak homiletically or not if only I could get people to see that Christ could meet every need of man, regardless of what that need might be. If we could see that, how wonderful the gospel would be! There is no need of going on half rations and serving God in our "poor weak way." If we get healed it will make us love the Lord more. When you get touched in your body naturally you want to love God more.

A Woman Restored to Her Family

I am a little slow to tell of healings in my own meetings so I will illustrate the point by telling someone's else. I never want to tell things for man's glory. A number of years ago my father was holding a revival meeting out in Connecticut. He prayed for the sick and afflicted from house to house—he visited them wherever they were. He would talk to people about it just as well as about their souls. He got a letter to come to Brooklyn, so he went there to hold a meeting. In the course of the meeting there someone told him about a lady by the name of Mrs. J. who was very much afflicted. My father went to see her. When he went into the home he found a very pitiful condition. The lady's husband would get up in the morning, make breakfast and get the children ready

for school, and carry his wife out and set her in the
chair, propped up with pillows. She was entirely helpless, all doubled up—her hands and feet were knotted
up with rheumatism and arthritis. He had to leave
her sitting in a chair. Neighbor ladies took care of her
between the morning and the noon meal. The children would come home from school and get a little
bite to eat and Mr. J. would come home from work,
do the washing and clean the house. They had two
children. They were out everywhere without a mother
to help them. They had nobody to make them mind.
They were very bad, and grew up on the street. The
neighbors would tell Mr. J. about the children and
they threatened to put them in the reform school.
The poor husband was heavy-hearted all the time. He
made $1.25 a day in the steel mills working all day,
and coming home to find his wife in a helpless condition. Christian people lived near there. They used
to come out and visit Mrs. J. and they would tell her
this was a blessing of the Lord. That man got so he
hated God, he had no use for Christianity. He hated
the God that he thought had made his wife sick. He
needed a mother to take care of the children. They
went on like that for several years, until my father
went into that home. Mrs. J. was afraid of him at
first. People are often afraid when you talk about
divine healing. Why? I am sure I do not know. But
when he went into the home he started to read out
of his Bible. The lady said "I wish you would read
out of my Bible because they tell me you have a
different kind of a Bible than we have." He said "All
right." He read out of her Bible and showed it to

her. First she could not see but that the Lord was making her sick for his glory. My father got her convinced of the mistake in that idea. Several times he went there and talked to her about divine healing before he felt she had faith to be healed. Then he said "Now we are going to look to the Lord for healing and you believe God will do it." He anointed her and laid hands on her and prayed for her. God instantly healed her. She jumped out of her chair and ran about the house praising the Lord. She clapped her hands. The thought that was uppermost in her mind was that God healed her so she could use her hands, she did not think about walking. She thought if she could only use her hands she could work. "Oh," she said, "I can use my hands." She moved her fingers. She was so happy. She ran into the court and the people came running out of the buildings. She was so happy she said "Oh, look, I can use my hands." The little girl came home from school and saw that it was her mother in the court. She ran as hard as she could run and said "My mamma can walk, mamma can walk." Crowds gathered in. One man happened to be near there, and that was in the days before Ford became so popular, and he had a bicycle. He saw what happened. He just went wild. He said "Something strange has happened." He said to everyone he saw that he knew that something strange had come to pass. He said, "Either Christ had come back to earth or else it was anti-Christ, one or the other." The crowd came. Someone got in touch with the New York World and sent a newspaper reporter out to see what was going on. The crowd

surged in there and my father was still there. The
reporter pushed his way through and got a testimony
from the lady, and he wanted to see the man who
healed her. They found my father. He took his hat
off as if my father had done it. My father tried to
tell them he did not do it. The whole country was
stirred because of that one healing.

Then this lady thought of the lady next door who
had wonderfully helped her. She ran down to where
this lady was and she went into the house and said
"Praise the Lord, God has healed me." This woman
was very quiet. She said "Let us not be too demon-
strative, let us pray." She thought she would get her
down to pray. She saw she could kneel and out of
the house she went praising the Lord. She came to
my father and said "I want you to stay and have
supper with us." In all of his ministry he said he
did not know of anything more touching than that
experience. Mrs. J. got the fire ready and got everything fixed up. They got the children all cleaned up
and got a big fine dinner. It was nearly time for
Mr. J. to come home from work. Everybody but the
family went home for supper. She said "I want to
surprise him now." They sat back in the room and
looked out and they saw him coming—he was lugging
his old lunch pail and was dragging along, coming
home as usual to find his children were disobedient
and the neighbors threatening, and his wife in the
chair—and perhaps he would have to do the family
washing and clean the house up and do the same thing
day in and day out. He got to the steps; they had
quite a few steps in front. As he reached the foot of

the steps Mrs. J. could not stand it any longer. She opened the door and stood there so her husband could see her. My father said Mr. J. took one look and saw his wife standing there, and she said "Papa, Jesus has healed me." That man just staggered, and fell up the steps and threw his lunch pail down. He reached in his pocket took out the tobacco and threw it down on the steps, and said "I want to give my heart to the God who has healed my wife."

Friends, you know I love to preach on healing because I find people want to give their hearts to the God who can supply every need.

V

THE CHILDREN'S BREAD

V

THE CHILDREN'S BREAD

I heard one man make a very foolish and unwise statement once. He said that there is only one verse in the Bible about Divine healing that we can take for our basis. He is mistaken. There are whole books of promises and chapters we might take for the basis of healing.

Tonight I will take a case of healing from the Bible. Matthew 15:21-28.

"Then Jesus went thence, and departed into the coasts of Tyre and Sidon. And, behold, a woman of Canaan came out of the same coasts, and cried unto him, saying, Have mercy on me, O Lord, thou son of David; my daughter is grievously vexed with a devil. But he answered her not a word. And his disciples came and besought him, saying, Send her away; for she crieth after us. But he answered and said, I am not sent but unto the lost sheep of the house of Israel. Then came she and worshipped him, saying, Lord, help me. But he answered and said, It is not meet to take the children's bread, and to cast it to dogs. And she said, Truth, Lord: yet the dogs eat of the crumbs which fall from their masters' table. Then Jesus answered and said unto her, O woman, great is thy faith: be it unto thee even as thou wilt. And her daughter was made whole from that very hour."

Now there are two things that I believe are necessary in every person's life who wants divine healing. The first one that is outstanding is the perseverance that the woman had. She pressed right on when Christ seemed to refuse even to answer her. The disciples did not discourage her when they said, Lord send her away. She pushed them out of the way and got to Jesus. Some people are very easily discouraged in seeking God for spiritual blessings, and many times they fail to receive what God wants them to have because of a lack of perseverance.

The Need of Perseverance

From the natural life we can show that men fail by the thousands unless they persevere. Those who succeed persevere. Some people are very easily discouraged. If they hear someone say a little word discouragingly or if some little word is said, and the devil will always try and find somebody to say that one little word to discourage you if he can. This woman had to push by the disciples. It is sometimes necessary to push people out of the way to get to Christ. Sometimes it is your own mother or your husband. You have to elbow them out of the way. They would put you on a side track—not willingly, but because of their unbelief that sometimes hinders. And we that are coming for healing of the body sometimes have to show a little perseverance or else we will fail to receive the blessing. I would say as Doctor S. D. Gordon said in his book on "Quiet Talks on Prayer," "The devil never surrenders any ground until he has to." God tested Abraham. We read in Gal. 3:5, "He therefore that ministereth to you the Spirit, and worketh miracles among you, doeth he it by the works of the law, or by the hearing of faith? Even as Abraham believed God, and it was accounted to him for righteousness." Friends, if we are going to have the working of miracles we must believe God as Abraham did and be willing to stand without any other evidence other than God's Word. God said so and that should be enough. We should be willing to

hold on to God's Word alone. I believe we need to
honor God by our perseverance in holding on to his
Word, and when God sees that he will see that we
believe, and it will be accounted to us also even as
to Abraham.

A verse of Scripture came to me very forcibly on
one occasion—the three steps in prayer. Jesus said
"Ask and ye shall receive, seek and ye shall find,
knock and it shall be opened unto you." Many people
get in the first stage—they ask. And then if they do
not receive they say I have asked for it and I do not
get it; it must not be the Lord's will; if it was he
would have given it to me. What we need is to pass
beyond the asking stage. Get to where you "seek"
it, and then go on to the final one and it shall be
opened unto you. Be determined and the doors will
open. Jesus said to the woman—"that we ought always to pray and not to faint." He couples prayer
with faith. He wants us to come and come determined
to get the blessing because of his promise. He has
been waiting for the opportunity to give it but we
sometimes must be determined to get it so the devil
will not keep us from having what God wants to give
us. Sometimes it is delayel. Daniel was twenty-one
days waiting for the answer. Nevertheless, God said
by his angel I heard you the first day and I came
because of your prayers, but the prince of the kingdom of Persia withstood me one and twenty days and
I had to send for help. If Daniel had given up in those
twenty-one days he would have lost the blessing.

That is so in human life all about us. A man in
Texas was drilling for oil. He felt that this particular

soil contained oil. He sent a sample to the government and had it examined. He took a survey of the land and said, "This land has oil under it." He started to drilling and got a few friends interested. They kept going down and down. He ran out of friends and money. He got the grocery man to give him credit. He mortgaged the place and everything. He went to another grocery store and got credit. Finally everybody withdrew credit. He was left alone except with what he had on hand. He kept on drilling until they went to the very last. He decided to eat dinner and then go and get another job and let the thing go by the board. After they got through eating his wife said that they could work a little in the afternoon. About the middle of the afternoon the oil spouted out in a great stream. He took his wide Texas hat and filled it with oil and put it on his head. He shouted, "I have struck oil." Everybody thought it was all right. Why can we not have the perseverance in spiritual things that the world has in natural things. If we could get the church of Jesus Christ determined in the same way the world is determined, the church would not be in the background but would be setting the whole world on fire for the Lord.

Determination in Prayer

If you are going to be healed there must be in your heart a determination to be healed. This woman did not have God's Word for it. All she had was knowledge that Jesus had healed others, and cast out devils, and she made up her mind therefore that he must do it for her. One man said ninety per cent of

prayer is stick-to-itiveness. Prayer for healing is never
real prayer until you have made up your mind that
you are going to get the answer before you quit praying. If it is right to pray for it then it is wrong to
stop praying before you get it. If it is right to start
praying for revival meetings and that souls will be
born into the kingdom, then it is wrong to stop praying or else it was not right to pray for it in the first
place. There must be a determination in our prayer
that will push us on through all difficulties regardless
of what they may be. I believe that if man can see
God's promise he can be determined that he will receive that blessing because of the promise.

"The Children's Bread"

The woman came to Jesus. She cried out after
him and pressed through. Jesus never answered her
a word but left her alone. She kept on coming. The
disciples wanted to send her away. Jesus said "I am
not come but to the lost sheep of the house of Israel."
Just that little word encouraged her and she said
"Lord, help me." And Jesus turned around, and for
a long time I could hardly recognize and harmonize
this action of Jesus with the Son of God. Imagine
Jesus Christ turning around to a woman who was
beseeching him, crying out after him, asking for help.
The disciples tried to put her away. Christ had
ignored her but she sought him, and then he turned
around and answered, "It is not meet to take the
children's bread and to cast it to dogs"—as much as
to call her a dog. She was a woman from Canaan
and a Gentile. People looked on the Gentiles as dogs

and these Canaanites and the people of the Gentiles
were looked down upon by the Jews. They were the
outcast, unclean dogs. Jesus turns around and speaks
to her in the terms that the Jews might look at her,
and says "it is not meet to take the children's bread
and cast it to dogs." Note, friends, in passing, Jesus
called Divine healing "the children's bread." Jesus
said at the Lord's supper, "This is my body broken
for you, eat." Friends as we partake of the bread,
the emblem of the broken body of the Lord Jesus
Christ, it is to typify his broken body for our body
—not only a spiritual need, a physical one. The blood
was applied to the spirit and the body was broken for
our body. If you want this bread, which is healing,
then just become a child of God and you are naturally
eligible to receive the bread. God will not withhold
that from you. He said "I am the bread of life."
My little child has a right to be fed at my table because she is my child. She looks to me to feed her
that bread. I would not withhold it from her, and I
do not believe God would withhold his bread from his
children. The surest way to receive healing is to be-
become a child of God and then you are entitled to it.

Humility Manifested

But he said "It is not meet to take the children's
bread and to cast it to dogs." She did not say "Well,
I am not a dog, I am just as good as somebody else
and just as good as you Jews." No, she never said
a word. There was perfect humility in that life and
she was willing to be called a dog and not to deny
it—willing even to be classed with the outcast. She

said, "Truth, Lord." Just as much as to say "I am a dog and am not worthy." No person ever receives it on his own goodness. You never could make it by your own works. It is because of his great love and tenderness, and compassion, and because of his promise.

I have known some people to miss divine healing because they thought they were so good God ought to give it to them because of their great goodness. One man was very slow about coming to the altar for salvation. He was a very nice looking fellow. He thought for a long time there was no need of his hurrying to give himself to the Lord because he would be so glad to take him, he would be such a beautiful specimen as a Christian, and so he waited. When he came to the Lord and gave his heart to God, God saved him but he called him to be a missionary and sent him to Africa among the heathen. That is as much as God thought of his good looks! God loves a poor outcast woman just as much as he does you or anybody else. You will never get anything from God until you are humble. Perhaps pride has kept more people from receiving a blessing from God than any other thing—ashamed to come boldly and confess Christ. He said "If you are ashamed of me, I will be ashamed of you."

The Syro-Phoenician woman did not say "No, I am not a dog." She was perfectly willing to be called a dog. She said "Truth Lord, but the dogs eat the crumbs that fall from the Master's table." And she said, "Just give me the crumbs—just a little bit, that is all; just what is left over, Lord." Jesus said, "Oh woman, great is thy faith." Mark the seventh chapter says of her reply, "For this saying go thy way." How great was her faith! One man made the statement, "Faith gets the most from God but humility keeps the most from God." Sometimes people have great faith but it is not balanced with humility and therefore they lose what faith they had in the first place.

We need humility if we are coming to God for a blessing. Let us have real honest humility, I do not mean, put on humility. If you have not that humility in your heart and life there is only one way to get it in and that is by "putting on" Jesus Christ.

First there was perseverance. She made up her mind that she was going to get to Jesus and get what she was coming for. As with Jacob of old, she wrestled with God and said "I will not let thee go unless thou bless me." It is the man who wrestles with God who gets the blessing. Second, there was her humility.

Hear her as she calls, "Oh Lord, thou Son of David." The second time she came she did not say the Son of David—she just says, "Lord." In the Schofield Bible there is a footnote here. "Addressing him as Lord she obtained an immediate answer. The first thing that must be in every life that is seeking God for a blessing should be confessing him as Lord and Master of that life." Now to confess Christ as Lord means to confess him as Master, as Ruler, as One who is taking full charge. If I confess him as Lord I am no longer to have my way, I am to let him have his way. If you want help and mercy from Jesus Christ, come and confess him as Lord first, then you are eligible for the blessing. We see some who would be very glad indeed to receive healing of the body without the healing of the soul. But the two go together. If you would try to separate them you would just cheat yourself. Confess him as Lord. Say, "I will let you have your way Lord; I will surrender my way and will to yours."

Surrendering Our Wills

Friends, salvation comes when we gladly and completely surrender our will to God's will. The source of all sin at the very beginning was the setting up of one person's will against God's will. The greatest sin in the sinner's life today is setting up his way and saying "I will have my way and not yours, Lord." Why should you not surrender your will and let God have his will? There is no reason for you to be afraid. My child does not have to say "I want my way because I am afraid your way would not be best for me." I know better what is best for that child than she knows herself. Therefore my will is best for her. And, friends, God's will and way is best for you, better than your own. If you could always have your own way, whatever you wanted, whatever you will to do, and over here God's will—God's will is better for you than your own. You could not pick your own way out as well as he could pick it out for you. His will is ten thousand times better than yours. If we could see that and believe it we would have no trouble in surrendering our will for his will.

VI

CAN WE BE ABSOLUTELY SURE ABOUT DIVINE HEALING?

VI

CAN WE BE ABSOLUTELY SURE ABOUT DIVINE HEALING?

The fact that there has been much uncertainty and some fanaticism connected with this subject does not invalidate the truth. It is one thing to stand up and make fun of the counterfeit—to get up and laugh at somebody else who is wrong, but that does not answer the argument. That does not meet the need of the hungry seeker who needs healing for his body. So we thank God for the privilege of preaching the Word of God in regard to the subject of healing for the body.

Will He Heal Us?

Now how can we be absolutely sure about Divine Healing? Is it a matter of guessing? Is it a matter of whether some of us get it or some of us do not? Is it a matter of lottery? Can we come with any degree of certainty? Many people stumble over this. One lady who testified here one evening said she knew God could do it, and believed that God had done it in many cases. She was a firm believer in the power of God and believed in the Bible without any qualification. But when it came to the subject of Divine Healing, she had a faint idea, a very poor idea of what faith was for herself. It is one thing to believe that Jesus Christ when he was here on earth healed the sick, but it is another thing to believe that he will heal you. It is all right for me to grant that you receive healing, but quite another thing for me to go and get healing for myself.

No "Possibly" or "Maybe"

Do we have to just come and ask the Lord to heal us if it is his will and then go away and wait there patiently and see if the Lord is going to do it, and if he does not do it conclude that it is not his will, and if we **happen** to get it we think that we **happen** to be among those that it was his will to heal? Surely we can not look at it in that way because there is absolutely no faith in such a position. We must have some way of being sure about it because faith is being sure. It is not thinking "possibly," or "maybe"; some way I know that God heals some people all right but God does not heal everybody, no! no! One person in particular who talks this way came to me, and he was absolutely sure that God would not heal everybody. I said, "Who does God heal, and who does he not heal?" He said "We don't know that." I said "In order to be healed we must have faith." He said "Yes." I said "How can we be sure of it if we cannot know?" Well, you know it was just a little while until he was not knowing where he was because if God will not heal everybody, who will come by faith and touch him, then how is anybody going to know?

Here is some Scripture along this line whereby we can be certain that God will do the work for you and me. If you are here with a sick body I want you to put yourself in and say "I can know it to be so." "Can we be sure about Divine Healing," was the thing that puzzled me when I first started out to pray for the sick. I said, "Supposing I go out and some get it and some do not. How will I explain it?"

I came to the place where I accepted his Word and I believe he will take care of his own Word.

A Test of Faith

Once I took sick when I was going to preach on the subject, can we be absolutely sure God is going to heal us? I was so sick when getting the sermon ready I could hardly see, but I said, "it is so anyway." It is good when we can say God's Word is so even if we do not get healed. I decided I would preach it even though I died right there. It seemed I had twice as many bones as usual and they were all aching. It seemed as though my neck was as long as a giraffe's and that it was sore all the way up. I was sick all over and I had not eaten anything. I announced on Friday night that I was going to preach on the certainty of Divine Healing. I got up to preach. I rocked in the pulpit. It was in the Cadle Tabernacle in Indianapolis. The people looked blurred moving before me. But God healed he that night while I was preaching. I went home and went to bed well. I slept well for the first time for a week.

God tests our faith. When we get to the place where we will believe Him in spite of everything we can be sure God will take care of His own. Many times we try it and if it doesn't work we run off on a pair of crutches. I would like to take the pair of crutches away—it is that "if." If we could get that "if" away what a wonderful time we would have. If folks did not have this old prop to fall back upon! When the "if" is there it is on your side and not on God's side.

Faith "the Evidence"

Perhaps you say, "I know some people who missed
healing," and "I know somebody who was prayed
for and he died." Yes, I know numbers of them.
Some have been prayed for and did not get a thing.
I can tell you of people who were baptized who went
down a dry sinner and came up a wet one. I have
anointed people and the only difference afterwards was
that they had a little oil on them that they did not
have before. Some people get water on them, they
are just wet, that is all. All who have faith in God
are saved, and all who have faith in God will get
healed. You say, "I have faith in God." Yes, but
have you faith for healing? Paul saw a man that had
faith to be healed. That is a different kind of faith,
to believe that God is able and then to believe that
He does heal right now. The Psalmist gives light on
this in the 103d Psalm. "Bless the Lord, O my soul:
and all that is within me, bless his holy name. Bless
the Lord, O my soul, and forget not all his benefits:
Who forgiveth all thine iniquities;" who healeth **some**
of thy diseases? Part of them? Half of them? Those
who are sick for God's glory, and if it is his will? No,
that is not right, but that is the way some people read
it and practice it. Who "forgiveth all" and "healeth
all." If we can not believe that "healeth" is "all"
how can we be sure that the "forgiveth" is for "all"?
There is no faith any way short of knowing that God's
promises are true. If I only believe God heals some
people I have not a bit of faith in the world. If I
say I will give everybody here half a dollar except ten
people, nobody would be sure of getting it. You might

be one of the ten. You could not be sure. You might think you would be the lucky one, but you might not be. You would not have faith. Faith is the "evidence."

When they have a court martial and have an execution in the army they have twelve men for the firing squad. They go out and pick up the gun. Every gun is loaded but one gun has a blank cartridge. Why do they do that? So that everyone of those twelve may think, "Perhaps I was one who had the blank cartridge; perhaps I did not fire the fatal shot."

There Must Be Certainty

If we are going to have any faith there must be certainty. People come just to try healing. You won't get anything if you come that way. Some say I saw somebody else get it and I am going to get it. You will not get it that way. You will get healing if you believe God's Word and believe it means you. "Who forgiveth all thine iniquities: who healeth all thy diseases." "Gracious unto all that call on him"—not just to some part of them, but to all of them. We have a right to claim it ourselves. His promises are yea and amen to some of those who believe? Is that right? To all! To all! To all!

We were in Kentucky holding a revival meeting. They brought a girl into the services who had a bad disorder. Her head was badly swollen. She could not hold her arms up. She could not hold her head up. A song was sung—"No, no; a thousand times no. Jesus will never say no." That girl, who was about 15 years old, went home. She said I heard a new song tonight,

"Jesus never says no." That was the only thing she could sing all the time. I wish we could see that Jesus Christ does not say no. If you will come with faith believing he will not say no.

Scriptural Promises

In the sixteenth chapter of Mark Jesus Christ gives the commission to the disciples, and not only to the disciples, but to their disciples and clear down to us. And he said unto them, "Go ye into all the world and preach the gospel to every creature." I love this verse in Mark. First it says to "go into all the world." That takes in this city. I am not willing to say it is all the world, but it is one part of it. It says to "go into all the world and preach the gospel to every creature." You are part of that "every creature," thank the Lord, and so am I, and we have a right to claim what is following here. "He that believeth and is baptized shall be saved." How many believe that? How many can be saved? Part of them? Some of them? No sir. To all the world, to every creature, clear down to this present time. They have a right to believe Jesus Christ for salvation. It is "Whosoever will let him come." Not part of you, not some of you, not a few of you. It is "whosoever." "He that believeth not shall be damned." The emphasis is laid on the faith, not the water. It is the "he that believeth not" that shall be damned.

"And these signs shall follow them that believe." It does not say the twelve apostles, it does not say the other seventy, it does not say some of the early church —it says "these signs shall follow them that believe," in one century or another century—man, woman, or child; bishop or wash woman—**them that believe.** Thank God. I am glad that is just like it is, that it is not for one or another, that it is for anybody who will believe—to all the world, for every creature.

"In my name." In the 14th and 15th chapters of John we find Jesus saying also, "Whatever you ask in my name I will do it." "Ask largely that your joy might be full"—"that ye might bear much fruit. Herein is my Father glorified." "They shall cast out devils in my name, they shall speak with new tongues; they shall take up serpents; and if they drink any deadly thing, it shall not hurt them; they shall lay hands on the sick, and they shall recover." How many? To all the world, to every creature. You can not read it any other way. The first is to all the world and every creature, so is the other to all the world and every creature. There is no doubt about it, no quibbling—brought to all the world to every creature. We are sounding out a whole gospel for a whole man.

"After the Lord had spoken unto them, he was received up into heaven, and sat on the right hand of God. And they went forth, and preached everywhere, the Lord working with them, and confirming the word with signs following. Amen." Friends, I don't know why it should stop. I cannot find any place where it says it is done away. But it is "let it be so" to all the world, to every creature, to the end of this present age. You and I have a right to it. You can be sure of it. If we can not believe God's Word along that line, what can we believe? If we are not sure it is

because we have not faith. Many are just on the fence.
If there is no certainty there is no faith.

Then there are other verses. In order that I might
get a person saved I must show him that Jesus Christ
said in his Word "Him that cometh unto me I will in
no wise cast out." That Him means whosoever, not
part of them. It does not mean occasionally, now and
then he takes them in; but whosoever will, let him
come. I have to get a person who wants salvation to
see that God will keep his Word, must I not?

Taking God at His Word

I was praying with one person for salvation, and he
was having a very hard time. It seemed very difficult
for him to believe that God would save him. He knew
God had saved people. I argued with him. I said
"Why would he not save you?" He said "I don't
know." I said, "He promised to do it." When I got
him to the place where he could believe, I said "Will
you believe he saves you?" He was almost afraid to
say it. He had been looking up to me. He said "I
want that feeling, I want that shout." "It is a case
of believing God and his Word, the rest will take
care of itself." Finally he said "I will believe Him, I
will take him now." It was not one minute before he
had all the joy he wanted.

One time while preaching I said, "Anybody who will
actually believe God—I am sure God will come into
his heart." I said, "Just come right up and God will
meet you before you get here." I looked in the audience, and back in the back end of the tent a fellow
stepped out into the aisle. He was a railroad man, the

hardest man down there. He had killed a couple of fellows in his early life in fights, and who should start to the altar but this fellow! Of all the hard-looking men there, he was the worst. When he started up my knees got a little saggy. I said "Lord, what did I say that for? I wish I had not said that, but you will have to make it real, Lord." He kept coming and I began praying with all my might. I said "Lord God, meet that man in Jesus' name." He kept coming a little closer. I said, "You said you would do it. Your Word is yea and amen. I believe you." As I talked to myself God came into his heart and be began to throw his arms around everybody. He shouted and praised the Lord. I am not against shouting of that kind. If it is not man-made and not in the flesh, it is all right.

In order to be saved a person must see that God will do what he said he would do. I have prayed for hundreds of people at the altar. Many would be in doubt, they would cry and hammer the altar. Nobody gets saved that way. When I forsook all and believed, the work was done. Right now it is done because we take God at his Word.

The "Any" of James 5:14

Healing is identically the same. We see God's Word. They both come as we see the promise and believe it. In James 5:14 the Word says "Is there any sick among you." How can we get anything but **"any"** there? It says is there "any" sick, let him come. How can we read in there that God heals some people but not everybody? Do you suppose God wants you to come and then makes fun of you after you come? No sir.

If "any" are sick, let them come. He gives the lesson of Elias who prayed earnestly. Would God tell us to come and pray like Elijah did for something he does not want to give us? No. If there are any sick among you "let him call for the elders of the church; and let them pray over him, anointing him with oil in the name of the Lord. And the prayer of faith shall save the sick, and the Lord shall raise him up; and if he have committed sins, they shall be forgiven him. Confess your faults one to another, and pray one for another, that ye may be healed. The effectual fervent prayer of a righteous man availeth much."

Friends, we have a right to come and claim that promise. Did those in the apostolic days consume all of God's power? No, thank God. We still have a right to come. You can include yourself in that "any." If you have a need you can say, "I am part of the 'any' and I am going to come to Jesus tonight." Should I say, "if anybody will come up here I will give you a healing card," then you have a right to come. It does not say "any" if you have done all you can do yourself. It does not say if you are old, or young, if you had it a long time, or a short while. Just "if any"! Man, woman, child, rich, good-looking, or anything else. "Any sick." What does it mean if it does not mean "any" sick? If we can not be sure of that we have no faith.

VII

WHAT IS FAITH?

WHAT IS FAITH?

"Nevertheless when the Son of man cometh, shall he find faith on the earth?"—Luke 18:8.

Now this perhaps has some reference to the general faith in the deity of Christ. No doubt you can see in it the reference to modernism and man's present day disbelief in the Bible, but if I read this with its context I am sure we will get another meaning entirely. Faith in God, in the general truths that are taught in the Bible, is not the faith that this has reference to primarily because the context shows differently. Many believe there is a God and they believe the Bible, and they believe Jesus Christ was the Son of God. Theoretically they accept it, but as far as experimentally believing it is concerned that is another thing. Now this I am sure has reference to something quite different, so I want to read the context beginning with the first verse.

"And he spake a parable unto them to this end, that men ought always to pray, and not to faint; saying, there was in a city a judge, which feared not God, neither regarded man: And there was a widow in that city; and she came unto him, saying, avenge me of mine adversary. And he would not for a while, but afterward he said within himself, Though I fear not God nor regard man; yet because this widow troubleth me, I will avenge her, lest by her continual coming she weary me. And the Lord said, Hear what the unjust judge saith. And shall not God avenge his own elect, which cry day and night unto him, though he bear long with them? I tell you that he will avenge them speedily. Nevertheless, (nevertheless, nevertheless, that nevertheless. Keep what has just been said with what is going to be said.) Nevertheless when the Son of man cometh, shall he find faith on the earth?"

A good many people come to us in regard to healing, and when we advise that it would be better for them to either read the book or to attend the instruction service they immediately tell us, "Oh, I am a Christian and I have all kinds of faith." A lady came to me today. I don't know whether she is here tonight or not, but if she is she will take this in the right spirit. This person was deaf. We ask all deaf people to read the book before being prayed for. She wanted to know what course to take to be prayed for. We told her to take one of the cards, read the book through, and come and be prayed for. She said, "I thought I could get it right away." I said, "No. We ask you to read the book." Faith comes by hearing and hearing by the Word.

Another person said to me, "I have all kinds of faith." I said, "How long have you been afflicted?" "Eighteen years." "And you have all kinds of faith?" "Yes." "And you are still sick?" "There must be something wrong with that kind of faith." Paul looked down at his audience and seeing a man, he said he perceived that he had faith to be healed. The faith this has reference to is that personal faith that believes God and takes things from God.

Preaching Without Practising

Naturally we cannot expect a modernist to have any faith—men who deny the deity of Jesus Christ, that do not believe in miracles. I have known many a fundamentalist who has declared himself—who would fight to protect the Bible. Some of these fundamentalists remind me of a man who went to a community. He

said, have you got many Christians here in town? Are
the churches well attended? The reply was, we have
people in this town that would die for the church and
for Christ, but not many who would live for him. It is
one thing to die for the fundamental truths and another
thing to live them and practice them and not just to
preach them only.

I said to one of our biggest fundamentalists—one
who has to preach against the modernist and the liber-
alist every time he gets into the pulpit, and make faces
at the monkey, "if any one wants to claim relationship
with the monkey, let them do so. I don't that is all."
This man would go in a tirade and fight for the Bible
and fight for the miracles, but when you talk about the
miracles of today he says it is all done away with. He
preaches it but does not practise it. He has perfect
faith in the Bible but not a spark of faith to accomplish
here and now what the Bible promises. . . . That is
the kind of faith that is scarce in the land. Is the Son
of God, when he comes, going to find that practical
faith that believes God for the things that we need?

Crying Day and Night

He tells us about a widow who came before the unjust judge. She could not get what she wanted at
first but came again. She came with the idea of getting the answer of being avenged of her adversary.
Finally she kept coming so long and so often that the
judge said, "because I was afraid that she will weary
me I gave her her request, not because I fear God."
Will not God "avenge his own elect," why cry unto
him once in a while? Occasionally? We say, "I want

so and so, Lord.'' If we get it, all right. If we do
not, we run away. Charles Spurgeon called it the
''run away knocks.'' He asked what would be thought
of a man who went up to a cashier's window at the
bank and presented a check and ran away. You would
say either the man is playing with the bank or else he
is a fool. People do just that way in religion. They
come to the window and present the check and go
away. It is those who go there and stay who get their
checks cashed. If you are praying and earnestly seeking something from God and have a determination to
win, you will get the answer. It is those who always
pray in faith and cry unto God day and night. What
is it that will make a man cry day and night and con-
tinually? It is faith. He believes he is going to get
the answer.

Scarcity of Real Faith

When the Son of man comes he is going to find a
scarcity of that kind of faith in the land. I want to
bring out of this a little practical lesson and thought
with regard to divine healing. There are thousands of
people who come to God and ask for something and go
away, and if they do not receive the answer immediately they get discouraged. Then they say, ''I was
prayed for the other night.'' They say, ''now my
stomach trouble is almost gone and my nervousness is
almost gone, but I had a little trouble with my ear
and it is not all gone. Shall I be prayed for over
again?'' They are willing to throw it down because
they did not get it all at once. If you will be reason-
able, friends, and look into this argument that I am
presenting I am sure you will see the logic of holding

on and the faith that perseveres and is determined to get the answer. "Hold fast that thou hast." Be determined that you are going to receive full and perfect healing.

Look not to Symptoms

Faith that will be active in your life and that will produce something is that faith that comes from a determination to get the answer. This faith is based on God's Word—because God says so, we believe it. Regardless of the results, we believe God's Word. God promised a son to Abraham. Paul wrote about it in the 4th chapter of Romans. Abraham was past that time in years and so was Sarah. No one in those times had known of such aged parents bringing children into the world. It is said "he staggered not at the promise of God through unbelief but was strong in faith, giving glory to God; and being fully persuaded that what he had promised he was able to perform. And therefore it was imputed to him for righteousness. Now it was not written for his sake alone, that it was imputed to him; but for us also, to whom it shall be imputed, if we believe on him that raised up Jesus our Lord from the dead." Now Paul writing about Abraham here describes and tells us how it was that Abraham believed God. God told him that he would give him a son. He did not look at himself and say "that is impossible." He did not look at the symptoms around about. He believed God. He believed that God was able to do what he promised. The promise of God to a sick person is this, "They shall lay their hands on the sick and they shall recover." If you have done your part you never need to stagger. If it does not happen in a moment, don't throw it all away and say "I thought sure I was going to get it." One reason we ask you the question on the healing card, "Is your faith based entirely and exclusively on God's Word," is because the symptoms do not always go away. We are looking at God's promise and not the symptoms. The symptoms make no difference whatever. Abraham looked to God's Word, not the symptoms. If you will look to God's Word you will believe God in spite of the symptoms. I believe that a person who has faith, one who has his faith based on the Word of God, could come and be prayed for and go out and feel worse and still know that God was going to heal him. Believe God even though you feel worse. We should get to the place where we can rest on God's promises and not worry. You never need to worry—if God said it, it will be so whether it looks like it or not.

Supposing I draw out some natural lessons concerning faith. There are some flowers—they have just been cut off from the bush. They look perfectly normal. They look as though they have life in them, but they have not; the leaves are going to drop off very soon. It doesn't look like it. But the source of life has been cut off. Numbers of people have their eyes in the wrong place. They look at outward manifestations. God is not dealing with the symptoms. God deals with the cause, not the effect. If you had the headache, God is not going to take your head off, he is going to take away what causes the headache. It may be spinal disorders, it may be stomach trouble.

One man was prayed for. I saw him the next day. I said, "How do you feel today?" "I feel worse as

far as feelings go, but I know God is going to heal me."
The next day he said, "I am worse, but I know God is
going to do it." I asked "how do you know"? "Because God said he would and I believe it." God told
Noah to prepare an ark, yet for 120 years the sun shone
and everything looked all right. All the antidiluvian
preachers were preaching sunshine all the time. I wish
people could believe God long enough to work for him
and stand on his Word 120 minutes. I said to the
Brother W. the third day, "How are you?" "I am
still worse. I know God is going to heal me. I am just
as sure of it as I am sure of my name." I said "praise
the Lord." The fourth day I said "How is it today"?
He said "I never felt better in my life, but I was just
as sure the day I was prayed for as I am now that God
was going to heal me."

Healed of Blindness

A man in Chicago was afflicted with blindness. He
was taken to the Mayo Brothers and they said he would
never see. The eyeball was shrivelled up. In Fort
Worth, Texas, he was grinding a little hand organ
playing, "Home Sweet Home." He got tried at something and began to swear. Something went wrong. A
lady overheard him. She spoke to him about it. He
said "excuse me for my language." She said "I
would like to have you go down to church with me."
He went. He heard the gospel message. He gave his
heart to God. After he was saved the thought came
to him, "If God could save me he surely could give me
eyesight." He said to his friend, "Could not God heal
my eyes?" She said, "Yes, I am going to ask him."

So he prayed and asked that God would give him eyesight. He had the assurance through God's Word that he would do it. He told everybody he met that he was going to get his eyesight. The next day he was just as blind as ever. The people thought, "the poor fellow is going into fanaticism." He said, "God is going to give me my eyesight." If believing God is fanatical, I will take my lot with the fanatics. I claim it is not fanaticism—it is the finest, most sensible thing in the world to believe God. He pecked along for several days, and went everywhere. If he would hear somebody walking near him he would tell them that he had been prayed for and God was going to give him his eyesight. They thought, "poor fellow." The eighth morning when that man awakened, he was staying in a brother's home, he said, "brother, brother, brother! What is that I see? Is that two windows and light up there?" He said, "point to it." "Yes." "There seems to be a little one over there." He saw the door transom light. You know that brother stood in one place not two feet square and danced for an hour, and praised the Lord. For seven days after he was anointed he was just as blind as he ever was. He could not see a thing. He said the only thing that he felt was a little burning in his eyeballs. But he said he was not thinking about that. He said "I saw God would do it and I knew I believed it." The last time I saw him he was in California, preaching the gospel. He said he could not preach, he was just telling what God had done for him. So many people said "I don't believe it," that he had to carry a record from Mayo Brothers to prove that he was blind!

Oh that we had a few more people who would just believe God's Word as it is and stand on it! Healing is not excitement, healing is not an emotion that we create, or a little wind that will blow out. No. Faith rests on God's Word. You can stand on the Word and believe God in spite of everything else no matter how it looks, no matter what people say—if you had a goiter it might seem to grow larger after you had prayed (and it always does if you look at it). One woman was prayed for and she said that every time she looked at it it got worse. She finally said she would believe God, and it went away.

Feelings Not Faith

Faith is not feelings, it is not sight. It rests upon God's Word alone without any other evidence. Pacific Garden Mission gave their converts this statement— "God's Word said it and I believe it and that settles it." Yes, that is all that there is to it. God's Word says that they shall lay their hands on the sick and they shall recover. The next thing for you to do is to believe it. The next thing to do is to let that settle it.

I said to one man (who had rheumatism) after I prayed for him, "stamp your foot and see how it feels?" He looked at me and smiled and said, "It doesn't make a bit of difference how it feels. God says that "they shall lay hands on the sick and they shall recover." That is good enough for me." I said "all right, go on." There was no argument or doubt. God said it, he believed it, and that settled it with him. That is believing God. Have you that kind of faith?

There is no worry about it—nor any excitement about it necessarily.

Resting on God's Word

When you come to God one time come for keeps and believe him, just rest. If it doesn't all take place at once, that doesn't change it. God did not say if you get well right away you will recover. He said they shall lay their hands on the sick and they shall recover. The devil says you will not recover. God's Word says you will recover. Some people say you will not. Will you believe God's Word or listen to someone else? Can you take God's Word and just believe it? Yes, you can if you will.

When I was first starting out praying for the sick I thought, "how can I do it? I have no testimonies of healing that I can tell. Nobody ever got healed in my meetings. I have nothing to tell the people." I was praying about it and did not know what to do. I opened my Bible to the tenth chapter of Romans and the 17th verse. "Faith cometh by hearing, and hearing by the Word." So today I am resting my case entirely on God's Word. This meeting and everything rests entirely upon what God says. Will you believe it? If you do, He will make it real. One person saw what God said while hearing preaching like this, and she said, "I will take it and believe God tonight." The thing was done, and that was all.

VIII

THE POINT OF CONTACT

VIII

THE POINT OF CONTACT

I want to show in this message: 1. That in the Bible people were healed differently. 2. That faith is different in some people. Perhaps we might attribute some of the healings that were different to the different degrees of faith. Jesus said of one person "He had great faith," and in another place "little faith." So we find faith can be in different quantities in one person than in another.

"Lay Thy Hands" and "If I May Touch"

To illustrate this truth I want to read of three cases of healing in the Bible. The first one is from the 5th chapter of Mark: "And when Jesus was passed over again by ship unto the other side, much people gathered unto him: and he was nigh unto the sea. And, behold, there cometh one of the rulers of the synagogue, Jairus by name; and when he saw him, he fell at his feet, and besought him greatly, saying, My little daughter lieth at the point of death: I pray thee, come and lay thy hands on her, that she may be healed; and she shall live."

Jesus said, "I will come and heal her. Thank God for his will to come and heal her. One point in this lesson that I want you to note is this: Jairus said "Come and lay your hands on her and she shall live." Jesus Christ went on his way to do as Jairus wanted him to, that is, to lay his hands on the girl that she might be healed—"And Jesus went with him; and much people followed him, and thronged him." The crowd was tremendous. "And a certain woman, which had an issue of blood twelve years, and had suffered many things of many physicians, and had spent all that she had, and was nothing bettered, but rather grew worse, when she had heard of Jesus, came in the press behind, and touched his garment. For she said, If I may touch but his clothes, I shall be whole."

One said "Come, lay your hands on her," and while Christ was in the act of going to heal the daughter, this woman who was suffering with the issue of blood for twelve years, said "If I can just press through the throng and touch but his clothes." The Gospel of Luke gives it "If I can just touch the hem of his garment."

Faith must have a point of contact before it is real faith. One said "Lay your hands on her." The other said "If I can just touch the hem of his garment"; she did not ask the Lord to lay his hands on her. "And straightway the fountain of her blood was dried up; and she felt in her body that she was healed of that plague. And Jesus, immediately knowing in himself that virtue had gone out of him, turned him about in the press, and said, Who touched my clothes? And his disciples said unto him, thou seest the multitude thronging thee, and sayest thou, Who touched me? And he looked round about to see her that had done this thing. But the woman fearing and trembling, knowing what was done in her, came and fell down before him, and told him all the truth."

Jesus, in that press, in that crowd, in that jostling throng! Now if she just hit him and bumped him extra hard there would be every reason why he would notice it; but he turned around and said "who touched my clothes?" The disciples in effect said, "You say, Who touched you with all this crowd jamming and crowding around— then you say, who touched me?" But Jesus said, "Somebody touched me."

Many people are jostling in the crowd and just a few are coming by faith and touching Jesus. After I go away from this revival meeting somebody will say, "How many people were healed." I can tell you exactly. As many as Rev. Erickson laid his hands on? No, sir. As many as attended the early 6:45 instruction service? No. As many as really get to God are made whole. Some are reaching out by faith and touching him. He said to the woman (it was not his faith, the faith of the Son of God—it was her faith) "thy faith hath made thee whole. Go in peace and be whole of thy plague."

I must read the rest of this. "While he yet spake, there came from the ruler of the synagogue's house certain which said, Thy daughter is dead: why troublest thou the Master any further? As soon as Jesus heard the word that was spoken, he saith unto the ruler of the synagogue, "Be not afraid, only believe.'" We find this ruler of the synagogue said to Jesus, come and lay your hands on my daughter and she will live. His faith would never have operated until Jesus came and laid his hands on her. His faith would not have taken hold; there was no point of contact until he saw Jesus lay his hands on his daughter—then his faith would have taken hold. While he was on the way to do it this woman who had this issue of blood said I

will just touch the hem of his garment, his clothes.
That woman had more faith than Jairus did, but there
is one thought that is the same. Just touch his clothes.
If she had missed the clothes she would have missed it.
Her faith operated from that point of contact. If she
would have missed it the first time perhaps she would
have tried it again. No doubt she had to press hard to
get to Christ, to get through the throng. She might
have had to push Peter out of the way. The Syro-
Phoenician Woman—the disciples wanted her out of
the way. Sometimes you have to push through the
crowd. Sometimes you have to push your relatives
aside, sometimes your preacher has to be pushed out
of the way to get something from the Lord. You touch
Jesus and you will be all right.

Both of them had a point of contact. One said "lay
your hands," the other said "if I can touch."

"Great Faith"

Here is another reference from the 8th chapter of
Matthew beginning with the 5th verse. "And when
Jesus was entered into Capernaum there came unto
him a centurion, beseeching him, and saying, Lord, my
servant lieth at home sick of the palsy, grievously
tormented. And Jesus saith unto him, I will come and
heal him." I love that statement. I have it under-
scored. The will of God! Jesus never turned any one
away. He will meet every need all the time. "The
centurion answered and said, Lord, I am not worthy
that thou shouldst come under my roof: but speak the
word only, and my servant shall be healed." That
fellow had more faith than all the rest. He gives the

argument. "I am a man under authority, having soldiers under me: and I say to this man, Go, and he goeth; and to another, Come, and he cometh; and to my servant, Do this, and he doeth it. When Jesus heard it, he marveled, and said to them that followed, Verily I say unto you, I have not found so great faith, no, not in Israel."

Different Points of Contact

But there was one thing about all three of those cases that is the same. One had more faith than the other. The first had the least, the second had more, and the third had more than the other two put together. It was not necessary for Christ to lay his hands on him—not necessary to touch him. He said, "Lord, you just say the word and my servant shall be healed." Jesus said, "I have not found so great a faith, no not in Israel." This is the point I want you to see—there must be a point of contact before we have electricity. There must be a circuit. There must be a point of contact before it takes effect. So with our faith in coming to God—there must be a point of contact; there must be a time when we believe the thing takes place. Some people say I am going to pray all night if necessary. It is not necessary, but if you say that, it will be. Your faith will not operate until after you pray all night.

A woman came to the altar to be saved. She cried and sobbed her heart out to God. I said "Can't you believe God will keep his Word? Can't you believe God will take you now? Look up and say, 'Jesus, I believe you will save me now,' if you have met the conditions.'' She said ''When I pray through.'' She could not get to the place where she could say, ''Jesus, I believe you, save me now.'' I said ''I want you to do it now. You have had your way for an hour and that is long enough for you to be stubborn and not believe. I want you to look up and sing the song, 'He takes me as I am.' '' She said ''He doesn't.'' ''He says he will.'' ''Yes, I know he will when I pray through.''

Mark eleven says, ''What things ye desire when ye pray, believe that ye receive them.'' **When** you pray, not sometime. Otherwise it is not faith if there is no point of contact. Believing God is going to do it sometime will not bring the blessing. When that lady got to the place where she was willing to believe he did it now—she might have had it an hour before she did. She was fully repentant and met the conditions, and was entitled to believe it the first minute when she met the conditions as much as she was an hour afterwards. You who come to God, believe now. You say that is wrong. That is believing you have it when you do not have it. And so it sounds. The Bible to man's wisdom is foolishness, it does not seem right. When you read that verse, ''What things soever ye desire, believe that ye receive them and ye shall have them''—(not that you are going to receive them) and ye shall have them. When you believe, it is no longer the horse ahead of the cart. You already have it when you believe. Faith is the substance of things hoped for, the evidence of things not seen. The man who has perfect faith has the goods on hand whether it looks like it or not. There must be a point of contact.

Believing Him "Now"

Sometimes people come and are prayed for. They go on. The results sometimes are delayed—maybe some of the symptoms linger on a little while. Symptoms don't change the thing. People say I am not healed but I am still praying for it. There must be a believing God for it. Exercise your faith and claim God's promises and it will be made yours. Just praying and asking God over and over again is not exercising your faith for it. Set a time for it—"Lord I believe you do it now." **Now,** not some day, but now, and you will get somewhere. Not any time, sometime, in the future, but right now.

Many people say the battle is hard and that they are going through a real test, but everything will come out all right in the end. There is no need of saying that, if God is leading, it is all right now. With God all things are in the present tense. If you go into a train and get into a tunnel you do not say, "We will come out all right." You are all right right then. If you are in a dark test, it is not going to come out all right—it is all right because God is leading. Let us bring them down to the present time. **Now** I believe; **now** I accept. **Now** I enjoy. **Now** I live. All three of these incidents teach the same lesson. Because of the faith being greater in the last the point of contact was different. One said "come lay your hands on her." Another said "If I can go up and touch him." One said "say the word." We ought to believe with the centurion, that man who realized his unworthiness—"I am not worthy, just say the word and that is all." If that man way back there in that darkened age could look up and see God's Word why can we not see it in this age. "He sent his Word and healed them and delivered them from their destructions." Ps. 107: 20. Delivered them; as well as healed them by His Word.

Gradual and Partial Healings

A lady came to the revival meeting we were holding apparently looking about to find fault with everything. Not much grace is needed to find fault. She was hunting for faults more than anything else. She said I am looking for some New Testament healing. I said "you ought to be able to find some." I pointed her to Dorothy Bradway who had been paralyzed over six years and God healed her. It happened to be a miracle, an instantaneous healing. I said "the girl had not walked for six years." She said "I don't know her." I said "I can't make you believe it, all I can do is to tell you of it." I gave her two or three arguments. She said "I can not see it." She said "a New Testament healing should be instantaneous and perfect and never come back." I said "Yes, that is fine." I quoted her a little Scripture. Jesus sent the lepers away and it said after they went they were cleansed. And the child that was spoken of to Jesus, of whom Jesus said, "Go thy way the child liveth." When he came home he inquired and they said he began to amend at the hour Christ spoke the word. Amend! What does that mean? Does it mean that it was instantaneous? Perfectly done, immediately? No. Gradually it came. Hezekiah was healed but it was several days before he had strength enough to go to the temple. That is the Old Testament you say. The Old Testament is just as good as the rest. Jesus prayed for a blind man, put clay on his eyes. The man went about and saw men walking as trees. If I could not tell the difference between a tree and a man you would think my sight was pretty bad. Jesus, the Son of God, touched him again. If Jesus Christ could afford to touch and pray again, do you not suppose you and I could pray the second time without going all to pieces? Here was not a perfect healing in the first instance, but as he touched him again he was made whole. It is, friends, as we see the definiteness of God's Word that we have something to stand on. Not a maybe, not a possibly, but "he sendeth his word and healed them, and delivered them from their destructions." We find in the life of Christ there were instances of healings that were gradual, and some partial. And in the fifth chapter of James where he speaks of healing, the Word tells us that "the effectual, fervent prayer of a righteous man availeth much," and then James tells us about Elias, a man subject to like passions as we are, and he prayed earnestly that it might not rain: and it rained not on the earth by the space of three years and six months. And he prayed again. He believed in praying again. In another sense I do not believe we should come and repeat the same request over and over again, but Paul in Philippians says "let your requests be known with thanksgiving." We make up our minds that we are going to have the answer, and start waiting upon God, and we believe him and thank him and worship him, and as we desire we believe that we are going to have what we are coming

for and not going to be defeated—it is then we can get
the blessing. I used to be afraid to preach this way.
I thought at first that if I would preach that not all
people were healed instantly it would detract and people would not look to be healed instantaneously. I find
it works the other way. I find when people see the
Word of God, and the more they know God will do
what he said he would do, the more instantaneously it
is.

God Honors His Word

Once I prayed for a man who was afflicted with
rheumatism. He was crippled up pretty badly. He
had a time getting up on the platform. After praying
for him I said "Stamp your feet down and see how
you feel." He looked at me and smiling he said
"brother, it doesn't make any difference how it feels;
God's Word said 'they shall recover.' God's Word is
good enough for me." He threw away his cane and
was healed. There was nothing exciting about it. "I
am not worrying about how I feel." We do not have
to be afraid of preaching the Word. God will bless and
honor his own Word. That is why we come here, because God will take care of his own Word. We are
sure about that.

In one place we prayed for a good many people
but did not see any results. I told the people, "you
are going to see people get healed." They did not
seem to believe me. Many people were touched but
never came back. The temptation was you better
have them testify right away. No. We are not basing
our faith in phenomena. Healing is so—whether people get it or not.

A man came in who was totally blind for eight years. Nothing seemed to happen after we prayed for him. I said it is so anyway. God will honor his Word. The next morning that fellow saw a light— he had not seen light for eight years. People were healed from that time right along. Many told it. It swept the place by storm. We prayed for one hundred and a hundred and fifty a night. He sendeth his Word. You can believe this Bible as it is. You do not have to qualify it and say it is a spiritual healing. You do not have to visualize and spiritualize it away. You can believe it just as it is.

IX

HAVE FAITH IN GOD

IX

HAVE FAITH IN GOD

Tonight I want to read in the 11th chapter of Mark beginning with the 12th verse.

"And on the morrow, when they were come from Bethany, he was hungry: And seeing a fig tree afar off having leaves, he came, if haply he might find anything thereon: and when he came to it, he found nothing but leaves; for the time of figs was not yet. And Jesus answered and said unto it, No man eat fruit of thee hereafter forever. And his disciples heard it. And they come to Jerusalem: and Jesus went into the temple, and began to cast out them that sold and bought in the temple, and overthrew the tables of the money-changers, and the seats of them that sold doves; and would not suffer that any man should carry any vessel through the temple. And he taught, saying unto them, Is it not written, My house shall be called of all nations the house of prayer? but ye have made it a den of thieves. And the scribes and chief priests heard it, and sought how they might destroy him: for they feared him, because all the people was astonished at his doctrine. And when even was come, he went out of the city. And in the morning, as they passed by, they saw the fig tree dried up from the roots. And Peter calling to remembrance saith unto him, Master, behold, the fig tree which thou cursedst is withered away. And Jesus answering saith unto them. Have faith in God. For verily I say unto you, That whosoever shall say unto this mountain, Be thou removed, and be thou cast into the sea; and shall not doubt in his heart, but shall believe that those things which he saith shall come to pass; he shall have whatsoever he saith. Therefore I say unto you, What things soever ye desire, when ye pray, believe, that ye receive them, and ye shall have them. And when ye stand praying, forgive, if ye have ought against any: that your Father also which is in heaven may forgive you your trespasses. But if ye do not forgive, neither will your Father which is in heaven forgive your trespasses."

God expects fruit off of us if we are to continue to live here. As Jesus expected fruit from this fig tree, so he expects fruit from you and me and if we do not bear fruit, then the question arises, Why should we be in the way of some one else?

Jesus cursed the fig tree, saying "No man eat fruit

113

of thee hereafter forever.'' Then he went into the
temple and drives out the money-changers. In the
evening he went out of the city. In the morning as
they passed by, they found the fig tree dried up from
the root, and Peter calling to remembrance the words
of Jesus said, ''Behold, the fig tree which thou cursedst
is withered away.''

Faith Is Not Noise

Jesus evidently did not curse the fig tree in a loud
tone of voice. He did not yell at that tree or jump
and wave his hands at it. All he did was to speak
to it, more than likely in a moderate tone of voice
because the Word says ''And his disciples heard it.''
If I barely whisper you say, ''I heard it.'' If I yell,
there is no need for you to say you heard it, it is just
taken for granted. I draw some observations from this
—that Christ did not yell at the tree but spoke quietly
to it.

Faith is not necessarily noise, and noise is not necessarily faith. I remember I saw—and I say it in all
kindness not putting myself up as an example—but one
man prayed for a sick man and commanded the devils
to come out twelve or thirteen times if I remember
rightly, each time he got a little louder. I thought he
would knock the person over. I thought he was going
to drive the devil out by knocking him out. If a man
would come quietly and have faith, he could say it in
a whisper and it would be just as good. If it is backed
up by authority it is not necessary for it to be said in
a loud tone of voice.

Natural Means Not Necessary

Jesus did not use natural means. He could have said "Cut the tree down." He could have said "There is no need of that, just cut all the bark around it and it will die of itself." Many people get confused about means. They worry about medicine and other physical helps. People say "God helps those who help themselves." Yes, that is the way a lot of people think and they help themselves to a good many things. But if God will help us only after we help ourselves, how are we to determine when we have done all we can do? We would have to try every doctor, try every medicine, and go the full length of all the sciences we have today, and then we would not know. It is not necessary to rely on natural means. Jesus could have used natural means, but he spoke the word only. And friends, we have his Word today as well as they had it then. It said "He sendeth his Word and He healeth them." And His word has just as much power as when he was here. If we could believe just his Word! We do not base our faith on symptoms. Healing is so anyway whether people get healed or not. If I see it in the Word, it is my business to preach the Word if nobody gets healed.

I talked to a Baptist preacher in ———— where I went to hold a meeting. He backed up our meeting there and they had their men over. The business men of the town had prayer meeting every night for the revival. One little boy had a tumor on his tongue and his tongue hung out of his mouth and bled, it was all cracked. He had a handkerchief tied around his face that he might hide it. They had a deadening medicine that they would put on it to deaden the pain. Brother ———— said "I looked at him and I wanted to pray for him for a year, but his father was a Catholic and I was afraid if he would not get healed the father would be discouraged with the Protestant religion and have no use for it." We prayed for him and be began to get well right away. The minister said "I was under conviction everytime I looked at that boy because I thought he might just as well have been healed a year ago as now." It was not our prayer—it was God. God's Word is so. I said to Brother ————, "You do not hesitate to preach salvation do you?" "No." "Suppose they do not get saved, does that change it?" "No." "Supposing they get saved and go right back in sin, would that change it?" "No." "Then why does it change the other?" God's Word is what we are talking about all the time. We have not been preaching our experience, neither just telling something that happened because we did it. Jesus spoke the Word and he is sending his Word today and he will heal us today if we believe it.

God Strikes at the Roots

Peter said, "Behold the fig tree, it is withered from the roots." Friends, God strikes the thing at the roots —not the symptoms. The symptoms may be the same for a time, but God deals with the root of the thing. When God speaks the Word, the source of life of the disease is cut off, but not always the symptoms. The symptoms are often worse after one is prayed for than before, but they do not change the case at all. God deals with the root of the thing. You might cut a cherry tree down—the cherries would still be just as red as ever they were, but the life of the tree has been severed and the cherries will soon wither away. So with symptoms. I am not saved because I feel saved; I am not healed because I feel healed. Believe in God's Word in spite of symptoms. I am not going to say I am well when I am not well. I say sometimes the symptoms act worse after being prayed for than before. Jesus went up to the boy who was demon possessed and commanded the devil to come out of the boy, and the devil tore him all to pieces and left him like one dead—worse than ever. Then Jesus took him by the hand and raised him up and he was all right. God strikes the thing at the root. When God strikes it will quit in a little while. Take a rooster and cut his head off—it will kick around worse than ever, but he will soon quit kicking after his head is cut off. So with diseases—they will soon quit kicking if God cuts the thing off at the root.

God Deals with the Cause

Man deals very largely with the effect, and God deals with the cause. Man tries to get rid of the effect but God deals with the cause of the thing and then the effect leaves. Jesus said "Have faith in God." He does not tell us to have faith in man. Many people miss divine healing because they have faith in man. Some only want one person to pray for them and they think nobody else will do. Their faith is in man and not in God at all. In the first place it is an injustice to the man who is going to pray for you, and in the second place it is an injustice to yourself to have your faith in one man. Naaman, the leper, came to Elisha who, realizing that he had his faith in man, said, "Go out and wash yourself seven times in Jordan." He did not even go out to see him. The best thing for some people is to have their feelings stepped on a little.

Faith the Gift of God

The Bible says,"Have faith in God," and the margin brings out a point I wish to emphasize for a moment. Instead of "Have faith in God," it is "Have the faith of God," or "the faith which God gives." You and I don't exercise faith in ourselves. We come and ask God and he gives us faith—gives us his Word and gives us the faith to believe it if we ask him to. Some people say, "If I could only believe." Just let God help you and you can not help but believe. You can not explain how you get faith—it is the gift of God and just comes to you. It is the faith which God gives. Then how can a man who is not a saved man, who does not want to be a Christian, get that faith that God gives? It is only as we surrender that we get that faith. Many people are looking to a man and trying to exercise their own faith. If you will look to God and ask him to put his own faith in you, it will be the easiest thing in the world for you to believe for healing. This is not natural. We live so much in the natural. So many of our actions—the things we do— are in the natural. We do them only as we can figure them out. We try to study the law of averages and to see everything ahead. When we come to God we must believe, not figure it all out. Suppose I have a cancer, and I figure out how the Lord is going to heal it. That makes no difference. Mrs. Erickson sang the song "He Knows How." Thank God, He does know how! Believe him for it and he will take care of the rest. Many times I myself have worried about the "how" and said "I don't see how it is going to be done." But that makes no difference. Let God do it his own way. All we need to do is to stand on his promise and believe him.

"Whosoever"

I am glad for God's Word. It means much to me and as I read it I want to appropriate it. I want to read on to the very end. "For verily I say unto you, that "whosoever." Remember it is not some—it starts with the word "Whosoever"—"shall say unto this mountain, Be thou removed, and be thou cast into the sea; and shall not doubt in his heart, but shall believe that those things which he saith shall come to pass; he shall have whatsoever he saith." There is a whosoever and a whatsoever in that verse. "Whosoever" shall ask "whatsoever." It is not for some few. God's Word along divine healing is not for an isolated case here and yonder, but it is the "Whosoever will may come." Whosoever will shall ask or come.

Believing Man

I had a singer with us who told a story of the way God had healed him. He said he was Assistant Pastor at Moody Bible Institute at the time and he had charge of the Camp-ground. He was out there and got a bruised hip and ribs, and he was very sick and sore with it. He could hardly get around. He said he went to the Lord in prayer about it and it seemed he could find no answer. And he said as he was praying it seemed as though a man's hand reached the Bible to him and said "Here is my Word." He said, "Yes, Lord, I see your Word." That verse came to him as he opened the Bible. "What things soever ye desire when ye pray, believe that ye receive them and ye shall have them." He looked up and said "That is just backwards. Believe I have it when I am still sore and everything?" The Lord gave him a little mental vision and opened his eyes to see.

He owed a thousand dollars to different people—$300 to one man, $75 to the grocer for a grocery bill, $100 to another man. So he went down to the bank where his friend was the President, and he went up to the cashier's window. Mr. J. was back of the teller's window. He said, "Mr. J. I owe a lot of money in different places. I would like to pay everybody off and only owe you." Mr. J. said "All right. How much is it?" "Altogether a thousand dollars." He said "All right." He pulled out some brand new crisp 100 dollar bills. Right away he said "The first fellow I will pay is ———, then I will pay the grocery man, and then the other man." While he was counting it out, he planned. He did not have it yet. He said "I will do so and so and so and so." It came to him, "if you believe that you are receiving it, if you believe man when you have not got it at all, why not believe God?" By faith we spend it in advance. If we can believe man, why not believe God the same way? You go to the Western Union and write out a telegram. You give them the money. You say "tomorrow morning J. will get the telegram." He does not have it yet, but you believe it and act it. If you can believe man, why not believe God?

Not Guesswork

Healing is not a guessing proposition. Healing is just seeing that God said he would do it, and then believing his promise—"What things soever ye desire when ye pray, believe that ye receive them and ye shall have them."

Let me ask you a question. If a man was to come to this altar tonight to be saved and he would say "I know you promised to save me, Jesus Christ died to save me, and I believe he will save me some time." Would he go home saved? No, he would not. But if he comes up and says "Lord I see you have promised to save me, I have met the conditions and have repented, and now I believe you do save me," he is going to go home saved.

In Hebrews we read "He that cometh to God must believe that he is and that he is a rewarder of them that diligently seek him." Friends, that we might believe God's Word! We would not be looking at symptoms and at man. We would see that it is God's Word. It is not this speaker who counts in anointing. In being anointed no man should depend on me—it is the act of obeying God that brings the result. "Faith is the substance of things hoped for, the evidence of things not seen." If you tell me you are going to give me a dollar tomorrow, I believe it between now and tomorrow, but after I receive the dollar I don't believe it—I have the dollar. After you receive it, it is not faith then—you have the blessing itself.

Necessity of a Forgiving Spirit

Then I must read the rest of this verse. "And when you stand praying, forgive, if ye have ought against any: that your Father also which is in heaven may forgive you your trespasses. But if ye do not forgive, neither will your Father which is in heaven forgive your trespasses."

Coupled with our praying—"What things soever ye desire when ye pray, believe that you receive them and ye shall have them," Jesus said, "And when you stand praying, forgive if ye have ought against any."

Friends, one of the finest ways I know to be sure of healing is to get a real forgiving spirit in your heart and life—the love of God even for your enemies, and those who abuse you—those who say evil things against you, and lie about you and do things you know are wrong. Get to the place where you can forgive everyone, and then come.

Jesus said "Love your enemies, pray for those who despitefully use you and persecute you." The best way I know to get to the place where you can be healed is to get where you can love your enemies, and not only that but when your enemies revile you and persecute you love them still. Why should this be coupled up with prayer for healing? A man can not have that forgiving spirit in his heart for his enemies unless he first has Jesus in his heart. It is not natural for a natural man to love an enemy. He only loves as he is being loved. It is only as we get Jesus into our hearts that we can forgive those who have despitefully used us.

So if you are wanting a blessing tonight, and if there is any enmity in your heart, get it out of the way. You say "I will forgive, but I won't forget." That is no forgiveness. Supposing God forgave you that way. If you can not forgive in the natural, ask God to give you the supernatural—Christ himself.

X

HOW TO APPROPRIATE DIVINE HEALING

X
HOW TO APPROPRIATE DIVINE HEALING

I want to deal largely at this time with the way we receive Divine healing for I think we should place as much emphasis on this as on any other point, because if you would put $1,000 to my account in the bank and would not tell me it would not do me any good. If you would not tell me how to draw it out and show me how if I did not know, it would do me no good. So if I merely tell you that God has provided healing without telling you how to receive it, I leave you just about as badly off as if you had not known about it in the first place.

Three Steps

Here are three steps to the appropriation of Divine healing. The first thing every man must realize if he is going to be healed is that it is in God's Word and not only that God can do it but that he will do it. Faith must rest on the revealed will of God and not in the power of God. As we said before, the power of God does not produce the faith—it is the will of God. A phrase that is used as much as any other, and people mistake it for faith is, "I know God is able." That is not faith. Faith does not rest on his power, it rests upon his will. The first thing to know is that the Bible teaches the doctrine of Divine healing. We must see that clearly if ever we want to get healed.

The Word Produces Faith

Romans 10:17 tells us that "Faith cometh by hearing and hearing by the Word of God." I used to think that unless I could tell a dozen cases of healing no one would have faith for healing. I found out it is the Word of God that produces faith for healing and not somebody's else testimony. People say, Brother So-and-So was healed—I am going to the same fellow and I will be healed. No you will not. Unless you base your faith on the Word you have no faith, you have just an expectancy. Faith cometh by hearing and hearing by the Word of God. In the 107th Psalm we read "He sent his Word and he healed them." We have his Word today. Let us read it and find out that is his will.

I will give a few Scriptures that we may know it is the will of God to heal our body. Mark 16:16; "They shall lay their hands on the sick and they shall recover." You have a right to believe that Word. James 5:14. "Is there any sick among you? let him call for the elders of the church; and let them pray over him, anointing him with oil in the name of the Lord: and the prayer of faith shall save the sick, and the Lord shall raise him up." That is the Bible. That is His Word, not my word—His Word. I need never apologize for it, or even explain it, I need not do anything with it, I just believe it.

John 14:13. "Whatsoever ye ask in my name." That is his Word—he said "I will do it." In the fifteenth chapter He says—"Ask what you will and I will do it." We want to see God's Word. I could give a dozen or fifteen or twenty more verses along that same line that we might take his Word and be healed. You must first get a vision of God's Word and then will yourself to be healed.

I can not get a poor pagan Chinaman to believe for salvation until I show him the Bible teaches salvation. I must first give him a foundation. It is just as fruitless to pray for a sick man until you have told him about Divine Healing and have given him a Scriptural reason to stand on. I prayed for a good many people I know did not get a thing in the world. One reason was because they had no idea about Divine Healing at all. I am surprised when I deal with the subject of healing and talk to people, and when people want you to make an exception of their case. They say "I would like to be prayed for right away. I am from out of town and can not get back very well. It is difficult for me." I say "I would like to have you all attend the instruction service that I might know you have faith for healing." They say, "If that is it, we have all kinds of faith." I usually find out it is all kinds—not the right kind. If you ask them if they believe God will do it they say, "I know he is able to do it," and that seems to be all they know about it. It is well when we are coming to ask God for the healing that we have God's Word that we can stand on because the devil will try us. Jesus used the Word, and unless we have it before us the devil will trip us up. If he doesn't some of your friends will, and it is a good thing to have the Word of God on hand. It is good to know you have "thus saith the Lord," and you can stand on that.

I think it was William Jennings Bryan who said, "Jesus said 'it is written'" and the devil said "it is written"—why can't God's people say it is written?" Why do we not have it in our hearts that we can say "It is written?" You can meet the devil's arguments by saying "it is written." Be thoroughly established in God's Word first.

The Conditions Attached

Secondly, every promise has a condition attached to it. You can not take a promise just out by itself and accept it unless you first meet the conditions. Someone said that there were 50,000 promises in the Bible. I do not know. They say all have a condition except one, that one is "The seed of the woman shall bruise the serpent's head." There could be no condition to that for it was the promise of a great God. But other promises have conditions attached to them. In John—"If ye abide in me and I in you, then ask what you will." This rests on whether you are abiding in him or not. Mark 11:24, "What things soever ye desire when ye pray, believe that ye receive them, and ye shall have them. And when ye stand praying, forgive, if ye have ought against any." Have a Christlike, forgiving spirit; that is the attached condition. Another condition is to believe. I read a sermon that was printed in a paper by one of the New York clergy, trying to disprove the Bible. He said "When I was a boy I was told that God's Word was so, and I started out to practice it. I saw that verse in the Bible that said, ask whatever you will. I said, "give me a bicycle Lord." I did not get it. That proved that the Bible was not so." Nonsense! His failure did not prove anything. He did not really read the Word, that was all.

I will not take time to go into many of the conditions. We have gone over them elsewhere in this book. The promises are to those who obey him. "No good thing will he withhold from them that walk uprightly." "Because he hath put his love in me, therefore I will deliver him." It is well to give him our love and our heart first. Some people want the loaves and fishes—healing of their body—and do not want to give him their heart. Surrender your heart first to him. Salvation is worth more than healing. Your healing will largely rest upon how you obey God. "The obedient, they shall eat the good of the land." If you need to walk in the light and obey God, you must do that before you can claim the promises. It tells us "If our hearts condemn us not then we have confidence." If you have condemnation you can not come with faith.

Supposing I go to a bank and borrow $100 for thirty days. At the end of thirty days I fail to pay the bank the $100. I go on and in about sixty days I say to the banker, "I am sorry I did not pay it, I was short. I meant to come in but I failed to do it. Now I am in a hard, close pinch and would like you to loan me another $100. Put it in one note and I will pay it in thirty days." He believes my story and makes out the note. Then I fail to come in at the end of that thirty days, but I pass on by and I forget all about it until another sixty days are over. I happen to see the man. He says, "How are you coming along? We did not see you." I say "I am sorry I did not get to pay the note. I was very hard pressed. I need money again. Loan me another $100 and fix up the note." How many times do you suppose I

could do that and get by with it? They would not
have faith in me because I failed and did not keep
my word to the bank.

Believe, and It Is Done

The last step is what I want to bring to you mainly
in this message, for it is the subject of the evening
—**How we might appropriate Divine healing.** If we
have first seen the promise, seen his Word, met the
conditions—then believe. Have faith and the thing
will take place. I want to give you just a little of
what I mean by believing God. This verse that I just
quoted in the eleventh of Mark says, does it not?
"What things soever ye desire when ye pray, believe
that you are going to receive them and you shall have
them." How many know that is so? If you do, put
your hand up. Well, it is not true. That shows you
were not listening. "What things soever ye desire
when you pray (not going to receive them), but what
things soever ye desire, when ye pray, believe that
ye receive them, and ye shall have them." Believe it
now. First we meet the conditions as we see his
promise, and then we believe he does his part. It is
the same with salvation. A man comes up and says
"I see your conditions Lord—'he that cometh unto
me I will in no wise cast out'—I come and surrender
my heart." He must believe that he receives him now.
Did you ever get saved any other way? You were
saved when you saw the conditions and met them,
and then said "Lord I believe you will do your part,"
and he does it, thank God, just exactly that way. If
you have met the conditions you must believe and

take it by faith believing. The trouble with so many today is we are afraid. We say "I don't feel any different." It is not a matter of feelings. It is receiving it by faith.

If we could only get people to praise God because he said he would do it, and accept him and his Word, and then praise him for it and believe it! It is just as you thank somebody else. Supposing Brother M. says "tomorrow I am going to give you $100." Well, I say "I don't feel any different; there is no use to get worked up about this thing, I haven't got it yet." I would not talk about it that way if I believed him. I would go home and be happy about it. I would believe because I am sure I am going to get it. A great many people, when coming to be prayed for, see God's promises and come happy as could be because they know God is going to do it. One man here said "I am thanking God for what he is going to do."

I was talking to a lady in Cadle Tabernacle who wanted to be prayed for without a card. Some people want to be different than anyone else. She said "I should not need a card, I have been a Christian a long time." I said "Do you know God is going to heal you?" She said, "Of course I don't know it." Another lady standing by said "Nobody can know it." I said "Then you ought to have a card and come to the Instruction Services." If you see God's Word you will know he is going to do it because he said he would. That is what faith is.

The Bible says, "Let the needy praise him." That means the sick man while he is needing healing. Praise him because he is going to do it. Is that not honoring

God? Certainly. The Word says "Let everything that hath breath praise the Lord." A sick man can praise him. A sister who was paralyzed could not talk, but she is praising God and her faith is increasing. If more of us would use our voice in praising the Lord more of us would get a voice.

I have made this statement before in regard to the question on the card about being convinced or about your faith resting entirely on the Word of God, and I will make it again without any qualifications. I believe if a man who is prayed for believes God's Word he can go home and feel twice as bad as ever and still know God is going to heal him. That is believing God because he said so, not because he feels it. Did you ever see any one get saved at the altar who said, "I don't feel any better?" They never get it until they believe, and then the feelings come afterwards. Let us believe it and then feelings will come all right. Suppose you weigh 100 pounds and don't weigh 200 the next minute—your faith must not rest on your feelings. Abraham believed God. He staggered not because of unbelief, the fourth chapter of Romans tells us. He considered that God was able and looked not to himself or to Sarah, but believed that God was able to perform what he promised, and he waxed strong when he kept his eyes on what God had promised. Some people look to see how they are coming.

Many people's faith rests entirely on feelings. "The just shall live by faith," not feelings. Faith will bring feelings, but feelings will never bring faith. Faith is not sight—it is believing without anything other than God's Word. I say **anything**. The Scriptures are the greatest thing in the world, they can not fail. You are believing something that never made a mistake. God's Word can not lie, it is infallible, and it will work wherever it is believed. As long as Peter kept his eyes on Jesus he was able to walk on the water. The children of Israel when bitten by snakes were told to lift their eyes to the brazen serpent hanging on the pole, which is a type of Jesus Christ—they were told to look at it for the healing of the body. If they could, back in that dark age look at the type of Jesus Christ and be healed, why can we not by looking at Jesus Christ himself? God wants you to look at him, not the symptoms. Disregard the rheumatism. If you hunt for it you will surely find it, you will get just what you are hunting for. One man had a stiff neck and was prayed for. He could turn it anywhere he wanted to in an instant. The next night we did not see him. We did not see him the second night or the third. On the fourth night he came back and sat way back in the house. My brother-in-law was having the testimony service. He said, "How is your neck tonight?" He held it toward the side as he did before. A lot of people said it would not last. Some predict that and then they will do everything in their power to keep it from lasting so what they said would be so, and some of them profess to be Christians too. He said "It all came back." He said "I have not seen you for a night or two." He replied "I thought I would stay home and see if it came back." My brother-in-law said "You got what you were looking for then, didn't you?" If you believe God, it won't come back; if you disbelieve it will come back.

There must be a gripping faith. Jesus could do no miracles because of their unbelief. When he saw their faith he said to the sick man, "Take up thy bed and walk." Believe God's Word in spite of symptoms.

Suppose Brother M. said "I will give you $100." You say, "Don't get confused about that, I know Brother M." It casts a doubt on it. I say, "He said he would give it, but the brother said he was not reliable." But if I have faith, I know Brother M. will do it. If I believe him, it makes no difference how many people say it is not so, I am expecting that $100 tomorrow. I wish he would say it, I would believe him! Why can we not believe God? Just believe it and receive it; not the symptoms, but his Word should be believed. Look at those old walls of Jericho —when the children of Israel went around them they shouted **before** the walls fell down, not afterwards. Many people are saving that shout to shout after the walls fall down, after the disease is gone. Shout before the walls fall. It is the man who has faith enough to shout in advance who gets the victory. If you believe him you will get a long way up the road very fast. Noah built his ark 120 years on dry land because God said there was going to be a flood. There were no symptoms of the flood. Many said "you are foolish." God said there would be a flood so he kept on working. If you are allowed to be tested, never be discouraged, just keep your eyes on the promise and you will be all right. If it is delayed a little while—it is not al-

ways promised that it will be instantaneous. There is
a difference between the gifts of healing and the gift
of miracles. A miracle is instantaneous. There is no
promise that we might be absolutely sure that it will
always be a miracle. The gifts were set up in the
church—the gift of miracles and the gift of healing.
Of some he said they began to amend from that hour.
It is as we can see God's promise to step out on it
that we find there is a certainty to it. I have observed
that the more people say "I dare to take it now," the
more they receive. Man by wisdom knew not God,
and man in humanly speaking does not understand
this Word at all. It looks puzzling. When you talk
about the Bible to them and the reality that there is
in God they think the Protestant and Catholic, and
the heathen religion, and the Confucian and Buddhist
religion are all on the same basis—just man's imagi-
nation, that is all. But we have proved and tested
that our God hears and answers prayer. If you have
had any difficulty in receiving healing, just say "I
will take it right now" and you need not wait to be
prayed for. You could be saved right out there in your
seat if you wanted to, and be healed also. Just look
up and say, "I do meet the conditions and I do believe." The work will be done.

We have some flowers here. They look just as
beautiful as they did on the bush, but the source of
life has been cut off. God cuts off the source of that
disease, and the effect will be gone. As we believe
God's Word the symptoms will all go away. Just
believe it and receive it by faith.

As I was preparing this talk it seemed a flood of

truth came into my mind and I seemed to see how little we have trusted God; how easily we have been satisfied with just a taste. One woman prayed that she might live over a certain Sunday, and then she was all right. Why could she not have asked for healing for a year instead of a week? The doctor said she would die in twenty-four hours. She just asked God that she might live until a certain Sunday— then she had reached the limit of her expectation.

"Herein is my Father glorified, that ye bear much fruit."

When Lazarus was still in the grave Jesus said, "I thank you because you have already heard me." If you and I can thank God because he has heard us and we know if He hears us we have the petition we desire of Him. Let us take Him at His word.

XI

SICKNESS THE CURSE OF THE LAW

SICKNESS THE CURSE OF THE LAW

"Christ hath redeemed us from the curse of the law, being made a curse for us: for it is written, Cursed is every one that hangeth on a tree."—Gal. 3:13.

Tonight, in speaking about healing, and having chosen this text, I have done it for this reason—that we might see what Christ did for us on the cross of Calvary. Christ, friends, means more to us than we have any idea. I like the statement of Dr. S. D. Gordon in his book, "Quiet Talks on the Healing Christ." He said "No man's hand has ever reached up to take all that the nailed pierced hand is reaching down to give." Christ, friends, has meant a thousand times more to us than we have ever had any idea. Our sister, here, has been a Christian for many years, but she had no idea that Christ meant healing to her. Christ hath redeemed us from the curse of the law. I am taking this in connection with healing. There is more than one thing that is the curse of the law, but sickness is one of them.

Sickness a Fruit of Sin

Some people look at healing in the wrong light. They think perhaps it is just a privilege that some have. Friends, Christ hath redeemed us—you and me, all of us, and we all have the right to come and take the healing that he has for us. Sickness is a result of sin. You say, well now I am not of that opinion because I know Christian people who are sick, and if it was a result of sin then why is it that Christians are sick? All sickness primarily came from sin. Until there was sin there was no sickness. So sickness is a fruit of sin. It is, in other words, a child of sin. There was no death until sin came, and sickness is incipient death, a slow death. A person who has a cancer or tuberculosis is having a slow death. And Christ, friends, has come to redeem us from the curse of the law.

One brother said "He scraped my sins all away." No, he blotted them out as scraping might have left marks. God came to take away the result of sin and bear the penalty of sin on the cross. He bore on Calvary the penalty of sin. He was made sin who knew no sin, and was made sickness who knew no sickness. He knew no sin—it was our sin. Christ on Calvary hath redeemed us.

Sickness Not a Blessing

Now before I go into what the curse of the law is specifically and definitely—what it was from the Bible —let me perhaps correct a mistaken idea that sickness is a blessing. Some have looked upon it as a blessing. They thought God was blessing them in some way. The Bible does not call it a blessing, it calls it a curse, a bond of affliction—that Satan has bound. Jesus said of the woman who was healed of the spirit of infirmity, "Ought not this woman, being a daughter of Abraham, whom Satan hath bound, lo, these eighteen years, to be loosed from this bond on the Sabbath day?" He did not call it a blessing. There is nothing about being sick for God's glory mentioned. I find many people today have a wrong idea in regard to sickness. They have petted it and humored it and thought God gave it to them to make them more patient and bring out some lesson. I grant that God has used sickness as a whip to punish his children when disobedient. But God is not an unjust God. If you will open up your heart and say I will obey you, then if it is a whipping God will take it away. Supposing I put a coat on my baby to keep her warm and she takes it off. I whip her and do not tell her why. Some people think God whips them year in and year out with disease. If it is a whipping, if you come and ask God he will tell you; and if you step up God will take away the lash.

I believe sickness is not a blessing, it is the result of sin. Maybe not your sin, but primarily it is the result of sin if we have to trace it back to Adam's sin. It comes sometimes by contagion—coming in contact with it in various ways. But sickness itself came as a result of sin. It is called the curse of the broken law.

What the Curse Is

If you want to find out what the curse of the law is, you will find it in Deuteronomy the 28th chapter. Then, when you read it, if you happen to have any one of those diseases named that I shall read you can say Christ hath redeemed us from consumption, or whatever it is.

"But it shall come to pass, if thou wilt not hearken unto the voice of the Lord thy God, to observe to do all his commandments and his statutes which I command thee this day; that all these curses shall come upon thee, and overtake thee."

The Word speaks about being cursed in the field,

but I want to deal with that in the body. The 22d verse, "The Lord shall smite thee with a consumption, and with a fever, and with an inflammation, and with an extreme burning, and with the sword, and with blasting, and with mildew."

The 27th Verse: "The Lord will smite thee with the botch of Egypt, and with the emerods, and with the scab, and with the itch." Some of you do not think that amounts to anything, but if you ever had the itch you would know differently. I had it and I know what it is. I want to itch now when I think about it. A man came to our home from Texas. He was a preacher. My father said, "stay over night." He slept with me in my bed. I got the itch from him. . . . "The Lord shall smite thee with madness, and blindness, and astonishment of heart. The 35th verse: "The Lord shall smite thee in the knees, and in the legs, with a sore botch that cannot be healed, from the sole of thy foot unto the top of thy head." The 61st verse: "Also every sickness, and every plague, which is now written in the book of this law, them will the Lord bring upon thee, until thou be destroyed." That takes in the measles the mumps and the flu and all the rest of the diseases of today as they come along. That is the curse of the law, and you have a perfect right to take your Bible and open it up to Galatians 3: 13 and say God hath redeemed me from consumption or whatever the disease may be. All other diseases not named in this book—Jesus Christ has redeemed us from all of them. He hath set us free. He bore them on Calvary for you and me. We do not have to bear the penalty of our sin—Christ bore it for us.

One lady when I was preaching said "Christ hath set me free; Christ bore it for me on Calvary." And her affliction left her. If Christ has set you free you do not have to call it a blessing. If it was a blessing you ought to ask God to give you more of it and not take it away at all.

Inconsistency of the "Blessing" Idea

I have known people who are inconsistent with their theory. They say "I believe God makes me sick because of his great love and because he is wanting to teach me some great lesson." Yet they go to the drug store to get medicine and try to get rid of it after the Lord gave it to them. If I send my little girl out in the yard after I put a coat on her and say "Daddy wants you to keep it on"; if she takes it off she is disobedient. If God wants you to have it, do not try to get rid of it. "Grin and bear it." Praise the Lord for it. If you want to be consistent with your theory that is what you would have to do. Friends, I do not believe it is a blessing. I believe what the Bible says—it is a curse and you have the right to be free from it.

Brother K. said to me, "Some people say you preach against medicine and they do not like you for it. I have come to the conclusion that if anybody has a right to take medicine it is you. You believe it is the will of God to be made well. If your faith is not strong enough to be healed you could take medicine." Anybody who believes that it is not God's will to heal would not have a right to take medicine because they would be working against God. If sickness is a blessing from God we ought to run all the doctors out of town and burn all the hospitals; they are working against God's work.

The reason I am saying this is to bring out the truth that sickness is not a blessing, it is a curse and Christ hath redeemed us. It is natural for you to come back with this thought in your mind, if Christ redeemed us from the curse of the law, bore our sicknesses on Calvary, why are not all Christians healed? That is a fair question. We welcome all fair questions. We do not want to argue. That is not our motive. Any fair question we will try our best to answer. Why are not all Christians healed? Let me illustrate.

Included all in the Ticket

My father had a friend who was a preacher. He was in evangelistic work. He held a meeting that paid him a little extra money. The Lord knows how to keep evangelists down. The Lord always lets evangelists go broke in the summer and at Christmas time so they will keep on working. If they had plenty of money they would go up to the north pole and go to a fishing hole and fish. If you do not believe it, just try it sometime. This meeting happened to pay a little over. He was very tired. He said to his wife, "We ought to take a nice good vacation." She said "Yes." They figured out that they would go to Chicago and get on a lake steamer that makes a five day excursion trip. All in all it was a five day trip. They figured out how much it would cost them. They got their tickets. They were so happy because they were going to take that trip. They got three or four chickens and cleaned them. You would know he was a preacher or

he would not do that. They got them fried up nicely.
They baked a couple of cakes. They fixed up one or
two baskets of lunch. They had to take a pile of pro-
visions that would keep several days. So they took
along some crackers and cheese. They got on board.
They were so happy. They relaxed. They left in the
morning about ten o'clock. At lunch time they got into
their state room and they opened up their lunch. They
ate nice fried chicken. It tasted very well indeed.
They went out on deck afterwards and looked around.
Night came around and they ate supper. Next morning
they again ate chicken. There was one thing they
missed. Everything was cold. They had no warm
cereal. They had nothing much to eat for breakfast.
They thought they would like a cup of coffee. Nobody
said anything. They drank water. They had a little
fruit along and that helped moisten up their food. They
were not going to complain. Lunch hour came around.
They were working still on the chicken and it was fine.
That night supper came around. Mrs. D. said, "I wish
that we had a nice warm dinner tonight, but we have
to put up with what we have." On the third day they
said "I almost wish we had stayed at home. We could
have nice warm meals." John said "We have to put
up with it." "We can not expect too much. We must
not be too complaining." So they ate some more dry
lunch. The next morning they could just barely stand
it. They were beginning to get around to the crackers
and cheese. They were munching away at the crackers
and cheese, and they would see people come up out of
the dining room with smiles on their faces, wiping off
their mouths. They would pass by the dining room and

look in. They could see the steam coming off of the coffee. John looked it all over. The fourth noon he counted up his money. He thought, "well it would help if we had one good square meal." He went to a passenger and said, "How much does it cost to eat down there in the dining room?" The passenger said, "Do you not have a ticket?" He said "It is all in the ticket." John D. could hardly imagine that. He went to the Captain of the boat. He said "What does it cost to eat in the dining room?" "Nothing at all; it is all included in the ticket." Here he was eating crackers and cheese as they did not know it was all provided in the ticket.

So many Christians are just eating crackers and cheese. They say we can not expect too much. We will just bear this disease and put up with it and eat dry crackers and cheese. The funny part of it is this, some people have not got enough sense—after they see that it is provided by Christ in the atonement —they still want to justify themselves, and still eat crackers and cheese. They can help themselves to that. As for me, give me the whole bill of fare just as it is—salvation with healing and everything. God has more than that for us. We have been redeemed and set free. Praise his Holy Name.

One fellow saw an elephant at the circus. He was tied. He was rocking back and forth. There was a chain around his hind leg. Someone slipped the chain off. He wondered what he would do. But he kept rocking back and forth. Finally he happened to pull a little too far and he noticed the chain did not pull and away he went.

I wish a few people would go a little farther. They say they are saved and filled with the spirit. They just rock back and forth and think they have it all. If you would pick up your foot and get out of the old rut you would find God has a thousand times more for you ahead. Why sit there and eat crackers and cheese and rock all the time? We are no longer under the old curse. We have a right to praise God and take what is coming to us. Do you not want your share? If you want to fight for crackers and cheese I will let you have them. Christ has already made propitiation for my sins. He has borne my sickness as well as he did my sins, and I am not going to forget one part of it, I am going to claim it all. The Psalmist David said "Bless the Lord, O my soul, and all that is within me, bless his holy name. Bless the Lord, O my soul, and forget not all his benefits, who forgiveth all thine iniquities, who healeth all thy diseases."—Ps. 103. All of them, on Calvary. Where did Christ do this? "Cursed is every one that hangeth on the tree." On Calvary. We are free tonight. I feel it in my heart when I think what God has done for us and why. We have been set free. We have a perfect right to all God has provided for us. He said, Come and drink of the water of life freely, not just a little bit. Why not have all of the gospel instead of just a part?

You and I have been redeemed. What does it mean? In the Old Testament we find all the types under the Old Testament are looking forward to Calvary and to Jesus Christ. That is the theme and object of the whole Bible, that one central thought

—Jesus Christ. You will find there that certain of the first born of the animals had to be redeemed. Some one animal had been slain for that one. It was redeemed. They used to take a scape-goat and lay sins on him and drive him without the camp. Jesus Christ was your and my scape-goat. He purchased our redemption on Calvary and we are redeemed tonight. We have been purchased by the life and death of Jesus Christ and on the cross he purchased you and I perfect freedom from all sin and the penalty of sin. Praise the Lord!

XII

THE USE OF MEANS IN DIVINE HEALING

XII

THE USE OF MEANS IN DIVINE HEALING

Many people are under bondage to the use of means in two ways. Some people feel it is absolutely necessary to have them, and then worry about it if they were to take some so that they are under bondage to the means. One man came to me, he did not have much faith, he asked this question, "If I am healed will I have to throw away these crutches?" I said "If God heals you and if you can walk without them, will you be running around with them?" He said "No I won't." "Then," I said, "don't worry about the crutches, you can get rid of them any time."

The Herb Argument

Some take the stand that the use of means is entirely necessary for God to work, and I believe they wrest the Scripture to get something to stand on; but I notice there are very few Scriptures they try to use and they are so poor they can not stand on them and they begin to use a certain line of reasoning. This argument is used perhaps as much as any —"God made the herbs and put them here for our use." If that is any argument that gives us permission to use any leaves and plants and even tobacco. Of course, they do not use that argument when it comes to tobacco. It is one thing to have it here in the form that it is and another thing to fix it up and cook it and stew it and put something else with it and make something entirely different, and take that.

Divine Is Not Natural Healing

I shall try to use Scriptural argument and draw a few lessons out of the Bible that will explain the subject of the use of means. I said to one man "You believe in Divine healing?" He said "I do. All healing is Divine whether through the use of medicine or not." There is a certain sense in which all good is from God and in that sense it is Divine, but it is not Divine in the sense that healing is Divine as that which comes from God is. There is a certain amount of healing in our bodies—natural healing. If you cut your finger, blood will rush through—and the healing is in us in that sense. When we speak of divine healing, it is the help we receive without and beyond nature. Many times people get beyond human aid—there is nothing in science that can help them.

This man went on to say that God blessed the use of medicine. Many times people have very little faith. They go to the hospital and pray God to bless the operation. Why not ask God to bless without the operation? If He can heal a man when an operation fails, why can not he heal before the operation, before the doctor takes the case and do it just the same?

The Place of Doctors and Medicine

You say we should pray about the medicine. One man said "the way I believe in Divine healing is, I ask God to give me good judgment in going to the right doctor and getting the right kind of medicine, and pray that it will be all right." That is not faith, because who are you going to give the credit to, the medicine or the doctor, or God? Medicine is a study.

I am not saying anything against medicine or doctors. Doctors have relieved suffering and medicine has done good. Anyone would be a fool to say it has not done good. Medicine will work on a horse the same as on a Christian—on a saint the same as on a sinner. Certain medicines are designed to work a certain way. They will work on an elephant if you could give him enough without any prayer at all, they would work.

I was talking to Doctor ——— in Indianapolis. He is quite a surgeon. He said he went out to have an operation on a man. The man said "I want to pray before you operate." The Doctor said "It is all right, but I am doing the operating and when you come out give me the glory and not God." That was his work. He studied to know how to do it. Let us give him credit for what he does. Doctors are not opposed to Divine healing as a whole for many see the Divine working constantly.

I was talking to Doctor ———. He said "Believe in divine healing? Certainly I do." The doctor said he operated on a man not long ago and turned him over to the interne to sew him up, but he lived in spite of it. He found out later he had a wife praying for him. Her prayers, he said, and not his work preserved that man's life. Many medical men are not opposed to divine healing. They are not in opposition to each other—one is simply higher than the other.

Shall We Discard Medicine?

People come to me and say "Shall I throw away my medicine?" I say "Do as the Lord leads you." I am not going to tell one without faith to throw it away. My business is to preach to you the better way —God's first and perfect plan and will for every life. God has his first best for those who will meet the conditions and have faith for it; he has his second best for those who will not come and get the first best. You can have the first best if you want it. Do not be satisfied with the second, but get the genuine divine healing.

Medicine does not bother me a bit. Some people think we are in opposition to it. I am preaching that God heals, and when he heals there is no use for medicine. It would be a foolish thing for a man to take it after he is well. Let God heal you and you will not have to worry about medicine.

The Bible and Means

In the Bible I find no place where Jesus used means for healing. He anointed the blind man's eyes with the clay. There was no power in the clay. The power was in God and not in the clay. Jesus merely spoke the word or laid his hands on them and they were healed.

Many say "God helps those who help themselves." They say God does not do for us what we can do ourselves. Do all you can for yourself first, and then when you can do nothing more, come to God. Then how am I to determine when I have done everything I can do? There is no way to know until after you are dead. If you take that stand you never could come to God for it because you never know. Maybe there is some doctor somewhere who could help you, but how do you know?

One man spoke to me about Jas. 5:14 and said that there we find that God gave us means to use. The Word says, "**anoint** with oil," not give a bath or soak with oil, merely anoint and lay your hands on them and the prayer of faith shall save the sick and the Lord shall raise him up, not the oil. The oil simply was a symbol or type of the Holy Spirit. There was no healing power in the oil itself. It was the prayer of faith and not the oil that saved the sick.

Mark 16 tells us about laying on hands. It was not the laying on of hands, it was God working, not the means working. Jesus did not use any means. I can not find that the disciples used any means. Peter said to the man at the beautiful gate, "Look on us. Silver and gold have I none but such as I have give I unto thee." He knew he had something. He took the man by the hand in the name of Jesus he told him to get up and walk. No means were used.

Various sorts of people come to meetings like this. One man said to me "I do the same thing only a little differently. I do not do it publicly. I sit beside the bed and I think and put my hand on the afflicted part and massage the pain away." I said "That is nothing like ours. We do not massage a thing away, it is just the prayer of faith and not some natural means used." I do not see Peter getting down and massaging him and working him all over. He said "In the name of Jesus Christ."

Paul looked and saw a man who had faith to be healed. If this man was sitting in the meeting and he got faith to be healed I know Paul must have been saying something about it or else he would not have had faith. "Faith cometh by hearing, and hearing by the Word." I do not believe Paul was telling them that the age of miracles was past because that does not produce faith. Then he said "arise" when he saw he had faith. He stood up. No natural means were used.

In all cases there was no use for means, there was no power in the persons who healed. Peter and James, after they healed the man at the beautiful gate said, "Why look on us as if we by our holiness caused this man to walk?" No. "In the name of Jesus whom you crucified." It is not means that God used for healing of his people; it is as Jesus said it would be —"in my name." That is the way we get it. Mark the 16th chapter said "In my name—they shall lay hands on the sick, and they shall recover." Praise the Lord, it is in his name. John 14—"whatever you ask in my name." John 15, "whatsoever ye ask in my name I will do it." In his name, not the means. Why not come for it in that way? If we are going to turn our case over to God let us come to God and give him the entire case. Some people miss healing as Asa missed it. He turned to physicians and it says he died and was buried. Put all your faith in God, not part of it. If I was going to have Brother M. build this building for me and have another man down here, and say I am going to have you build this building, I would do both of them an injustice. Put all of your faith in God, not half. It will take all the faith you have, you have not any to split up and divide around with some one else.

A Praying Physician

A county surveyor, in one of our revivals, a prominent business man, had a daughter who was sick with diphtheria. She wanted to send for us to come and pray for her right away. The mother got all worried and excited because her daughter was sick with diphtheria, and we were away and could not be found. Mr. ——— came home. He said "Let us wait until Brother Erickson comes and have prayer." The mother said "No, we must have the doctor." They got a doctor, a member of one of the leading churches and a very fine Christian man. He thought God must work through him and could not do it alone. He prayed and asked God to help him to do it and give him proper judgment. No doubt he did that many times. He came and gave the girl an injection in her arm that was intended to drive the fever up and drive the disease out. He said "I am sure it is diphtheria." But he took a swab—to test it. She begged him not to give the injection for she wanted to be prayed for. He said "No, we will give you this." In about an hour after the doctor left they got in touch with us. We went over to see her and anointed her and prayed with her. The father was there and sat by the bed. In five minutes that girl had no more fever at all. Her temperature was normal, and she began to sing. She told her daddy she wanted something to eat. The mother was excited and did not want to give it to her, but they finally gave her something. The doctor was not satisfied with the test and so he came back to get another sample to test. We met him and had a little chance to talk with him. He went over to her and said "I would like to take another test, Helen." She opened her mouth. He looked in and was puzzled. He did not know what to say. The fever was gone. He said "I am sure it was diphtheria." Not a trace of diphtheria could be found when the test was made at the office. The doctor came back to tell us about it. He said "I want to talk to you." That man came just as humble as a little child. He was honest. He began to talk about Divine healing. He said "I do not understand it." That man today is a believer in Divine healing and practices it in his own town in California. The daughter of the Pastor of the Methodist Church took sick with lung trouble. He tried to work with her but could not do anything for her. He said "There is only one thing to do and that is to pray." The doctor got together with the father and they prayed, and God healed her. Thank God for people who will have open minds.

God did not use natural means; in spite of them he did it anyway. He did not allow the medicine to take its natural course. If God can take nothing and make something out of it, why can he not take something and make nothing of it? Instead of using the medicine for something he reversed it and sent it back and drove the fever down. God is not dependent on the use of means. He can do it himself without anybody else. He alone has power to do it.

People are struggling over these things—good, honest people who are conscientious and all that, but they have not yet seen the privilege of stepping out wholly on God's promises. So many are like Moses in the Old Testament. He could not go out alone, he said, "Send somebody else to talk for me." Let us not depend on any other thing. God is not limited that we have to go down to the drug store and get medicine and shake it before we take it, and pray God it will work all right. God is able to do it directly.

XIII

WHY SOME PEOPLE MISS DIVINE HEALING

WHY SOME PEOPLE MISS DIVINE HEALING

We will grant you that some are missing healing. Some folks come up to be anointed. We are minus a little oil, that is all they get out of it. There is no healing power in that oil any more than in the water. The blessing comes as we obey God.

Lack of Faith

Now, taking that for granted, I want to analyze why some people miss divine healing. First, I believe I could answer it in a few words—there is a lack of faith. That is the one great reason. There are a thousand and one reasons why we do not have faith. I want to consider some reasons why we miss it and I want to throw the blame on myself as much as on anyone else. It would not be fair for me to find fault and tell you why you miss healing without being willing to take some of the blame myself. The disciples failed on one occasion. They tried to cast the demon out of the boy and were unable to do it, and if Christ had not happened along some people might have taken that case as exceptional and by it try to prove that it was not God's will to heal everyone. But Jesus comes along and heals the boy and casts out the devil, which shows that it was a lack of faith on the part of the disciples rather than the will of God not to heal. So now there may be a lack of faith on the part of the "elders." We will take the blame first. The disciples had their eyes on the fierceness of the demon possessing the boy rather than on

the power of God. Sometimes that is true today. We
see that the case is very difficult. We say, "This is
a cancer, goiter, or consumption," and we look at
the hardness of the case more than the power of God.
I would say like Elisha, "Open their eyes that they
might see." Nothing is hard when you get a vision
of God and his power. All things are possible with
him. We will take that for the first one—that inci-
dent of the failure of the disciples is recorded in the
17th chapter of Matthew and the 20th verse.

A Community Lack of Faith

I want to take another one and bring it down
more to you and this city and wherever we live.
There is many times a community lack of faith that
hurts a revival meeting. It is a marvel to me that we
have as many miraculous healings as we do with as
much unbelief as we have in the world today, and
you do not have to go down to the pool rooms to find
it, you find it in the church.

I was talking to one of the biggest fundamentalists
in the country. He would fight for the Bible and just
storm around, and say wonderful things about the
Bible and less from the Bible than any other man
I ever heard in my life. I said "Why is it you men
who are fundamentalists exercise no more faith sometimes than the modernists? Why spend all the time
fighting for the miraculous in the Bible when you
deny the miracles of today?"

So we have a church and community lack of faith.
The world has been taught that the days of miracles
are over with and that they no longer exist. Jesus,

in the 13th chapter of Matthew said in one place he could do no mighty miracles because of their unbelief. If the lack of faith would hinder the Son of God as divine as he was and as all-powerful as he was—if it would keep him from working miracles, how much more would it hinder common, ordinary people like you and me. He said he could do no mighty miracles in a certain place save that he healed a few folks. I will differentiate between healing and miracles. Healing is a process; miracles are instantaneous. Some things are almost always miracles, and some things almost always healing. Some people miss healing because they are looking for a miracle and if it does not happen miraculously they miss the healing. We are not always promised that it would be a miracle, but we are promised that it will be a recovery. If I weigh 100 pounds I can not find a promise that I will weigh 200 pounds in one moment, but I am promised that "they shall lay their hands on the sick and they shall recover." That is God's promise and I can stand on that. Because we believe in divine healing that is no sign that we throw sense overboard and go blindly on. The miraculous happens as we can get a community faith stirred. It is noticeable that more miraculous healings happen as we go on. The meetings continue to get better all the time.

Faith Based on Miracles

So some people miss the healing because they are looking for a miracle. One man came and after he was prayed for he almost cried. Tears began to well up in his eyes, and I said "What seems to be the trouble?'' He said ''I just expected it in an instant, right when you prayed for me.'' I said ''You expected it did you?'' ''Yes.'' ''Did you know you would be healed?'' He said ''I expected to get it.'' ''What made you expect to get healed?'' He said ''I saw everyone else getting blessed and healed right along and I thought if they can get it I surely ought to.'' Faith rests on God's Word; expectancy rests on other things. He happened to have catarrhal disease. The eustachian tubes were stopped up. That has to go away before the hearing comes. If I am standing on Brother M.'s foot I would have to go away before he would get relief.

Some things are miracles and some things are healings. I prayed for one man. Later I asked him ''How are you?'' He said ''I am worse.'' I said ''Praise the Lord.'' He said ''Sure, praise the Lord. I know God will heal me because he said he would. It makes no difference how I feel.''

No Hindrance of Unbelief

In one place Jesus went in and put everybody else out because of their lack of faith. Then he raised a child from the dead. If unbelief hindered Christ it will hinder us. I have prayed sometimes when it seemed that my prayer was fighting me and I could not get it across. The air seemed full of darkness. The first week of a revival is hard sledding. You are praying up against something. People have been taught that the age of miracles is over. I talked to a minister not long ago in this town. He is a very fine man, one of the best men in town. When it came to divine healing he readily admitted that the church failed to preach divine healing as much as it should, and that it is not developed like the other part of the gospel. God wants a whole Gospel to be proclaimed.

Many times it is a lack of faith in the homes of the people prayed for that causes the sickness to come back. One lady in this meeting was a subject of prayer. Her home people talked to her and discouraged her. It took the woman's faith away from her in a moment. She was discouraged and will not come back. God wonderfully touched her body but she got where there was a lack of faith and she became bewildered. It would be well for you if you want healing to keep close to somebody who is trying to exercise faith.

Casting Away Confidence

I want to turn with you for a moment to Hebrews 10:35; "Cast not away your confidence which hath great recompense of reward." What is your confidence? That is your faith, is it not? The Bible says "This is the victory that overcometh the world, even our faith." One trouble with some people who miss divine healing is this, they cast away their confidence if they do not get entirely and perfectly well the minute that prayer is offered on their behalf.

Every one of us is tested sooner or later. Abraham was tested. God gave him a son in response to his faith, and after Isaac came and Abraham saw in him the fulfillment of God's promise, God said, "Take him out and offer him up as a sacrifice." Abraham went. He knew that the boy was the only channel God had in fulfilling that promise. He reasoned it out this way, God is able to raise him up out of the ashes. That does not change it. He can destroy all the evidence, but God said it would be so and it will be so because God said so.

People often throw away their confidence the first time they have a little rest. They say, "I thought surely I was going to be healed." It is not a "thought sure," it is knowing when you see it in God's Word. There is no uncertainty about it.

Never cast away your confidence. Many a man has lost perfect healing by simply throwing over his confidence in God. When Daniel was praying, the angel said "I am come because of thy prayers, but the prince of the kingdom of Persia withstood me one and twenty days; but, lo, Michael, one of the chief princes, came to help me; and I remained there with the kings of Persia." He was delayed one and twenty days—three weeks. God said he had to send his archangel to help him beat back the devil and bring the answer. The answer is delayed sometimes. If Daniel had given up before the twenty-one days was over, he would not have gotten the blessing. Even if the answer is delayed never throw your confidence away and say I guess it is not for me.

I very seldom tell stories. But here is one that I believe will fit in. A little boy heard that God made man out of mud. He thought he could do it if God could. One day after a rain he made a nice little mud man—he had it all done but one leg when his mother called him for dinner. He reluctantly went in. In the meantime another little boy came along and saw the mud man and kicked it out in a pond of water. The boy came out after dinner. The mud man was gone. A couple days later the boy was down town. He saw a one legged man. He followed him all around. The man got tired of it and said "Boy, why are you following me around?" He said "Why did you not wait until I got you finished?" A lot of people hobble off before God has finished His work upon them. Many people limp off on that "if it be thy will" and throw away their confidence when if they would wait a while God would complete the work he started to do.

"Need of Patience"

Notice now the 36th verse. "For ye have need of patience." What is patience? "That, after ye have done the will of God." What is the will of God for a sick man? To be anointed and prayed for is it not? "For ye have need of patience, that, after ye have done the will of God, ye might receive the promise." "They shall lay their hands on the sick and they shall recover." Never throw away your confidence because you did not quite get the full answer to your prayers. Just wait and God will give you the answer in his time.

Covering Up Sin

Another reason for missing healing is that people cover up sin when they come for prayer. "He that covereth his sins shall not prosper," infers that if we shall uncover our sins we shall prosper. How many people we have seen who said on the card "Yes, we

have been born again,'' when they know they have
not. Are you habitually committing any known sin?
They say "No." You can cover up that sin, and I
will not know the difference. All I can do is to make
the way as plain as I can for you. You must be
honest with God because he does the healing. You
could fool me when you say "I am saved," but it is
God who does the healing. I am not a healer any
more than I am a Divine Saviour. It does not make
me a saviour because some people get saved, nor does
it make me a healer because some get healed. So
people miss it because down in their heart they are
covering up sins and they are afraid to acknowledge
and admit it. Many people say I think I will get by
all right, I will not surrender my heart to God.

Those who do not confess their sins to God and
are not willing to confess them before men and make
a public confession of what they need of Christ fail
to have much faith when they come. "If our hearts
condemn us not then have we confidence toward God."
If I lie about a Brother, whether he knows it or not,
something condemns me. When we come to God we
know he knows. Why should we attempt to deceive
him or anyone else?

Turning to the Wrong Source

Let me turn to a man who failed in seeking healing—King Asa. (2 Chron. 16:12.) "And Asa in the
thirty and ninth year of his reign was diseased in
his feet, until his disease was exceeding great: yet
in his disease he sought not to the Lord, but to the
physicians. And Asa slept with his fathers." Friends,

if more people when they are diseased and in distress would turn to the Great Physician, the Lord instead of turning to the world, perhaps they would not have to have said of them as it was with Asa, "he slept with his fathers." He did not seek the Lord, he turned to the world to find it and failed.

The Unstable Man

James 1:6 tells us about the unstable man. He will receive nothing from the Lord. Some people are so unstable they are up one day and down the next. They are like the men "serving the Lord in their poor weak way." Let us get God to establish our goings.

Selfishness

James says "Ye ask, and receive not, because ye ask amiss, that ye may consume it upon your lusts," that is on nothing but a selfish desire. Many people want to get well just to get well—to save having to pay doctor bills, or for so much medicine. That is fine. I would be glad to save people money. One question we ask is, do you seek healing for the glory of God? The true motive that should prompt every desire in coming to God should be to glorify Him with the answer to prayer, and not just for a selfish reason. The best way to come to him for healing is to want to glorify God with that healing, and then it will be for the glory of God and for his interest to heal you.

God doesn't heal people to go out and serve the devil. He heals them to serve him. If you want healing in your body give God your heart first. We should

not ask God to take the work of the devil out of our
body and keep the devil himself in our heart.

My father was once dying of consumption. He
weighed only 135 pounds. Now and before he was
afflicted he weighed 200 pounds. He made up his
mind that he would have to die, but he did not want
to. He had six children, I was the eldest. He prayed
thousands of prayers that he might be made well.
All he could think of was that he had six children
to take care of which was a good legitimate reason.
He prayed and prayed and prayed and never seemed
to get anywhere with healing. He made up his mind
to preach with the flag flying at top mast. In a big
meeting in Massachusetts he heard some missionaries
talking about the great need on the mission field.
His heart was stirred. He was moved for the heathen.
He went home. He had been having night sweats and
immediately wrapped in a blanket. He said "I will
pray for the heathen in Africa regardless of how I
feel." He began to intercede for a lost world. He
forgot all about himself. He got beyond his own
family, beyond his children that he would leave or-
phans. In the midst of prayer he forgot about the
night sweats and the coughing, and was completely
lost in intercessory pleading for a lost world. The
Spirit of God prayed through him. A voice came to
him and said, "This would be a good time to be healed
so you could preach the gospel to them." And God
healed him in a moment. It was not for a selfish desire. Since that time he has gone to England and
Wales and preached the gospel. Now he is well and
strong and preaching the gospel today. When he got

lost to his own need and interested in the needs of others, he saw the glory of God. I think it was under Luther or Wesley—a great worker lay dying. God's leader got down and prayed. He said "Lord he can not die. He is needed for the work. Your work would suffer without him." He wrote him "You shall not die, you are needed in God's work," That man lived. It is recorded in history. If we know it is for the glory of God we are more certain to be healed.

In closing—perhaps I have not touched your reason. Maybe it is just a selfish desire. Maybe you would like to be well so you could work to take care of your family. Get beyond that and be well for the glory of God. Jesus died on Calvary and by his stripes we are healed, that he might be glorified in your spirit and body. If you want it for that reason, you need not wait for our prayers. You can just look up to God here and now and get healing.

INSTRUCTION SERVICE DISCOURSE
No. 1

INSTRUCTION SERVICE DISCOURSE NO. 1

The object of the Instruction Service has been to instruct people how to believe for Divine Healing. We find there are many who have mistaken ideas about it, therefore we have had this early service that people might get a thorough Scriptural foundation and may be able to receive what God has for them.

Not Fanaticism

People mistake divine healing and confuse it with fanaticism when really it is not fanaticism because after all is said and done healing is nothing more or less than believing God will answer prayer. That should be sufficient for us in time of need. If we are in need of healing we have a right to call on him and to believe that God answers our prayer. It is not by emotionalism, getting excited and trying to pray —just pray, that is all. Faith is simply believing God. Faith for healing is the same as it is for any other blessing—as it is for salvation. We find the promise, the Scriptural foundation for it, and believe it and accept it and that is all.

Faith Based on the Word

No man can have faith for anything unless he sees it in God's Word. "Faith comes by hearing." Rom. 10:17. "And hearing by the Word." That is one reason why we tell very few instances of healing in other

cities. Faith does not come by hearing about somebody else receiving it in some other town, in Africa,
or in China. I was reading an article not long ago
that appeared in the Sunday School Times, a very
conservative paper. They heard where a man had
been healed of leprosy in the Orient, and they wrote
to three different mission stations near and they
asked the missionaries to investigate thoroughly and
send them a written report of the case, and they did.
The Sunday School Times printed the story of the
healing of the man with leprosy and told all about it
and then gave the three missionaries' names and what
they said about it, and they all said the same thing
and all magnified God and they told how many scores
of people had given their heart to God and the heathen
had accepted Jesus Christ as a result. It started in
this way. There was a woman who came to the mission
station and was told of Christ and she accepted the
Word. She found a great joy in her heart, and she
argued thus "If God could save me, this same gospel
that could save my soul, means that I might intercede
with Jesus for my husband who is sick with leprosy
and he could be healed." And that is a good argument. If God can do the greatest miracle of all miracles, forgive our sin and take out the stony heart
and give us a heart of flesh—if we can be born again,
that is a miracle.

Miracles the Foundation

Doctor Evans made a statement. "No man can be
a Christian without believing in miracles because we
must believe he died and rose again and that is a

miracle." So our very foundation is a miracle. To deny miracles we would do away with many of the precious truths of the Bible that we hold most dear, and without these there would be no foundation for the gospel.

Not Contrary to Science

Doctor William Mayo made this statement, "I have often seen a preacher come in and do more in a moment than I could do even though I had done everything in my professional power." This was published not more than two months ago in the N. E. A. Service, and in the city papers here no doubt. I was talking to a doctor, one of Indianapolis' best surgeons. He said he was constantly being confronted with the miraculous, constantly in touch with the Divine. He said "I have operated on many persons and given them no hope of living, and they lived anyway. I can only attribute it to God." So miracles are not contrary to science—it just merely admits that God is greater than sickness and greater than disease. We do not deny disease—or say we are well when we are not well. God is greater than the disease and if we will trust him he will bring us out of the disease more than victorious for he says "If you will ask anything in my name I will do it." Not we will do it. We have never tried to make anyone feel we were the ones who did the healing. Faith rests only on the Word of God. If I were to tell you regarding salvation only about somebody who was saved in Africa it would not produce faith in your heart for salvation unless I gave you the Word of God that you can be saved. Wherever you believe it, God can work. God's way of working is to send his Word, and wherever it is believed he will do what he said he would do.

Excitement Not Necessary

Now we have at no time tried to create excitement. You will bear me out in this—those who have been here all the time. I am not of a very excitable nature myself and we do not try to work ourselves up to a high pitch where we are going to claim something we have not already received. If we meet the conditions we can stand on them regardless of how it feels. I feel saved because I am saved. If I was to rest my faith only on my feelings I would be saved half of the time and the other half I would not be saved. Some folks have a thermometer of feelings and if you happen to strike them when they don't feel so well they have not quite so much salvation. I am saved today because I believe in Jesus Christ and have met the conditions, made the confession of Christ and accepted him. After I am saved the feelings all take care of themselves. It is the same with healing. Meet the conditions and believe God that he will do for you according to your need. The Bible promises that he shall supply all our needs. If you have a physical need, why not claim a supply for that need just as well as for any other need? If God can raise finances in answer to prayer, sends the money to pay our church debts, why can he not send healing in answer to prayer for the body?

"Without Money"

We have a little card that we give to those who want to be prayed for. It costs you nothing to get them. One person told as authentic that we charge fifty cents for healing cards. That person has not come here because never at any time have we collected any charge. Elijah said "Is this time to receive money?" We never associate money with salvation or healing—they are the free gifts of God. If God gives you healing why should we charge? We would be getting money under false pretenses if we charge you for something we can not do. It is God who does the work if you are healed and you give God the glory. If you found somebody who came for healing who did not get it, he only came as far as the evangelist. One man was holding a revival in a city the second time. He met a man who was staggering drunk. He said "You don't know me do you? I am one of your converts." The minister said "You look like some of my work, if God had done it you would have been different than that." If you see somebody limping off on crutches, someone going back to the Pool of Bethesda, that is some of my work; but if you see somebody going on healed, that is God's work, not magnetism, hypnotism or auto suggestion. Healing is different than that. Many people have prayed and did not expect to get the answer to their prayer. It is just like talking over the telephone without anybody being at the other end. Suppose you give me a check. I go to the bank in the morning and I write my name on it and present it at the bank at the cashier's window and go away without waiting for the money. You would think I was foolish. People do that with the Lord. They write out their needs, they say I need help and strength. They leave it at the cashier's window and never expect to get it and would be surprised if they did. If God told us to come he would not tell us to come that he might make fun of us.

An Ordinance for the Sick

James 5:15, "The prayer of faith shall save the sick and the Lord shall raise him up." That is an ordinance set up in the church. Some people try to do away with ordinances and say they are no longer necessary. That is not so. They are set up in the church, the New Testament church has an ordinance for the sick. God did not tell us to do that in order to make fun of us. Surely if God asks us to come he means what he says. He has not said that to entice us on as some persons would do—who say "If you are in need I would be glad to loan you $50." When you go to borrow it they say "If you had hit me any other time—I just paid my taxes." I sympathize with you and you tell them how sorry you are. God does not do that. If he told you to come to him and pray he will do what he said he would do and will supply each one of your needs. All our needs are met in Jesus Christ. When he came down from heaven he came to bring back to man what the first Adam lost. In the second Adam we find what the first Adam lost —we find health in Jesus Christ. Christ is our salvation, Paul tells us. Then if you have a need today, come and have that need supplied in Christ. Christ wants to meet your need. Go to no other place for it— go to Christ. He is just as able today and just as willing as ever. Our faith can not be based on his ability. Our faith must rest on his revealed will.

Christ Willing to Heal

Perhaps there is one thing that is causing more lack of faith than any other thing, the devil has succeeded in blinding people's eyes to the revealed will of God, not to his power. God is a thousand times more than just able to do it—he is willing to do it. If I had anyone question me, I would far rather they would question my ability than my willingness. If you came to me and said "I lost my home, I am destitute, and am without food, and I know you are able to supply and give me food if you will do it" —I would far rather such an one would come to me and say "Now I know you will do it if you can." I would rather have them question my ability than my willingness. Yet with Christ, we never question his ability, but whether he will or not. Jesus Christ is just as willing as he ever was. The days of miracles are not over, and as I was saying a moment ago, Christ can supply every need. When the multitudes came and were without food the disciples said "Let us send them back to the city that they might buy food." Christ said "What shall I do with them because I have great compassion on them?" The underlying thought was his great compassion—he wanted to reveal God's love. Many people today are turning away from Christ and turning to the world to find the supply for that need when Christ can be all that we need. We don't have to seek it in the world no matter

what that need may be. In the life of Christ they
were in want of food. Christ supplied it. They were
in need of healing and Christ healed them. Christ
always met every need. Will he not supply every need
today as well as he did then? Can we not today in
this better age, in this better time have him supply
our needs? Jesus said it is better for you that I go
away. If it is as some would believe it—they are just
as conscientious and it is with no idea to put myself
up when I say this, but they just have felt that it was
done away with and Christ heals no longer. Jesus said
it was better that he should go away. How is it that
it could be better? It is better in this way—that when
Jesus Christ was on earth he could be in only one
place at a time. Only those who were in the immediate vicinity might touch him and be made whole.
But now he is everywhere and everyone of us can
touch him by faith and all can get healed whether
in China, Africa or right here. Anyone can reach out
by faith and touch him. When Jesus Christ was on
earth in Galilee, only those in Galilee might touch
him. They had to go across the sea and hunt for him
and they could only find him in one place. Now he is
with us always even unto the end of the world or to
the end of the age, that is, down to this present time.
Anyone can touch him by faith and be made whole.

"All Who Believe"

After this meeting is over somebody may ask how
many people were saved and how many were healed?
I will be able to tell them just exactly how many.
Every one I prayed for? No. All who came to the

altar? No. As many as believed on Him and touched Him were saved and healed. That is just how many. No more, no less.

Explanation of the Card

From night to night we have tried to lay a Scriptural foundation for faith. Many times we brought in a good many Scriptures. We preached on it two nights a week, Mondays and Fridays; and every night dealt with this subject in the early service. Now this card has a few questions on it. Let me briefly run over them.

The first question asked is "Have you been born again?" I would not have any feel that we are basing healing on a high level and salvation on a lower level, that we make the matter of the body first and the healing of the soul second. It is your soul that is far more important. If we pray for you and if you get healed, you will die within a hundred years from now but your soul lives on forever, and your soul is as much more important than your body as eternity is longer than time. And even though you never got healed, if God would save you you would be repaid even for coming to this service. I have seen many people who were Christians and sick and infinitely happy, and they died and went to heaven. I have seen sinners who were well but perfectly miserable and they died and were lost. We try to make everyone see we are making salvation first above everything else. We ask you if you are habitually committing any known sin. The Bible says "He that is born of God doth not commit sin.'' We have no faith in any experience that justifies sin.

Do you spend time each day in Bible reading and in prayer? One thing this revival meeting has done is that it has gotten many people to reading their Bible. If there is any need that Christians and church members have it is a need of reading the Bible. We find and I have noticed many Sunday-school Superintendents and Sunday-school Teachers who only read one chapter a week and that is the Sunday-school lesson. Then we have another class of people who we might term as Chapter-a-Day Christians. They read a chapter every day and I can almost always tell you where the chapter is—it is one of the Psalms because they are such nice short chapters. Just a little bit of a chapter the last thing they do at night. After everything else is done and you are ready to go to bed and sleep you read a little chapter and make God last and the world first. That is just the opposite to what the Bible says. ''Seek first the kingdom of God and his righteousness, then all these things will be added unto you.'' If you want to be healthy spiritually, read God's Word and pray and get in communication with God. Then you will be healed.

Are you harboring an unforgiving spirit toward anyone? The true essence of religion is love to Jesus Christ and to your fellowmen. We have at no time preached theology or creed—we are preaching love and Jesus Christ. We don't believe it is possible for us to have love of God in our hearts and hatred for our brother at the same time.

We ask you if you have any restitutions to make

or wrongs to right. We believe as Paul said that we should have a conscience void of offense toward God and man. If our hearts condemn us not, then have we confidence toward God. There are five questions on the spirit side. They have nothing to do with healing only as they hinder or make us to be in a position where we are eligible for healing.

The sixth, seventh and eighth questions follow. Are you convinced that it is God's will to heal you? Before anyone can have faith he must find out God's will and then believe intelligently. "If" implies a doubt and faith is not doubting. When I come to you and I say "If you will," I don't know whether you will or not. Faith is absolutely knowing and there is no way I can see how we can know until we first become convinced of God's will. "How am I to do that?" you say. Am I to have a special revelation or feel any supernatural, extraordinary feeling or ecstasy? No. You find it out by reading God's Word. His Word is his will. Have your faith based exclusively on the Word of God, not on us. Don't look to us in any way, shape or form. Look to God. It is not the one who does the anointing, it is not the man that baptizes. I believe in both. It is your obedience to God that brings the blessing, not the particular person doing it. It is the act of obeying God and being anointed that brings the blessing.

Do you seek healing for the glory of God? Your desire and motive when seeking healing should be that God would be glorified with that healing. One girl frankly told one of the workers—she was to be prayed for. She walked on a cane. They asked her why she wanted to be healed. She said "I want to dance like the rest of the girls." God heals no one so he can serve the devil. If you want it, want it for the glory of God. James says, you "ask and receive not because ye ask amiss, that ye may consume it upon your lusts." Just selfishness. The true motive is when we want to glorify God and will glorify God with healing and that brings healing.

Press Forward and Claim It

As we come, let us come expecting God to do it because he said he would. If I would tell you if you would come up on this platform I would give you a thousand dollars, many would come quickly and running, you would not come whining and crying and teasing and begging. You would come up because you believed you would get the money. It is very noticeable when we find people with faith and when they have not faith. When there is faith there is praising God because of what he is going to do. When there is not faith there is a teasing, a repetition— over and over again. It is because we fail to believe, otherwise we would ask and then praise him for it.

XV

INSTRUCTION SERVICE DISCOURSE
No. 2

INSTRUCTION SERVICE DISCOURSE NO. 2

We have this service here in the early hour each evening for those who want to be prayed for that they might have heard the Word of God and through the hearing of the Word might receive faith. There are thousands of good Christian people today who have not faith because they have not been taught along this line.

God's Will

One man said to me today, "Why is it that many Christian people are sick?" I said "For the reason that they have no faith." "Why is it they have no faith?" he asked. "Because they don't hear things that will produce faith along that line." As we went into the subject I asked him—he was also sick and wanted a little instruction—I asked him "Are you a Christian? Have you prayed for healing?" He said "Yes." "Did you expect to get healing?" "I did not know; I only prayed." "Did you pray that God would heal you if it was God's will?" He said "Yes." I said "that is the reason you did not get it." His eyes got big and he wondered why. That one phrase is keeping a good many people away from healing —"If it be thy will."

The Episcopal church after making a study of divine healing for three years with Bishop Reese at the head of it (they studied healing from every angle, took it from Scriptural facts, studied the Bible, put all things together and made a report to the church),

and this is their conclusion: "We find that when
Jesus Christ was here on earth he went about healing
all that were sick as a revelation of the will of God
to man for all time." And then they used a little
phrase that I wish we could embody in our experience,
"And we no longer can pray with that faith destroy-
ing, qualifying phrase, 'If it be thy will.'"

People have mistaken that "if it be thy will" for
humility. They have taken that thought and they
have been supposing that it represented real humility
when it is simply an excuse for a lack of faith. Just
saying "if it be thy will" and then passing on because we do not receive the healing. We say the Lord
did not want us to have it. It is simply a lame excuse
for our laziness in faith—some of us. Sometimes we
mistake the laziness of faith for the rest of faith. We
are too lazy to exercise our will and determine to have
it.

Determination Necessary

Now healing is the same as any other blessing—
we must first see the conditions or rather the promise
and then meet the conditions to that promise and then
be determined to have it. I have known people who
have prayed for revival meetings and never had them.
You have known of revival meetings that were not a
success. They prayed and asked God for it.

I was talking to a certain person today. He said
"I prayed for it, why did I not get it?" Have you
been in a revival meeting where they asked for a
revival meeting and did not get it? Yes. No prayer
is real prayer until you have made up your mind to

get an answer. If we are going to have a revival there is an absolute certainty that we can have one if we are determined to hold on until we get it. It might not come in ten days or a week or a month, but if we hold on it is an absolute certainty. So it is with healing, if we will meet the conditions and hold on. In fact faith is born out of a determined will to have what God has promised and not to be defeated by any spirit of the devil or any other circumstances; be determined that we are going to meet the conditions and then defy the devil, and we will get the answer. Then faith is coming because it comes out of determination.

And friends, with healing there must be a determination for us to receive the blessing. See the promise and then believe it and then never be satisfied until we receive it.

Healing a Certainty

Now, in regard to healing, there is no reason why we should look at that with any uncertainty; no reason why we should guess at it and puzzle about it and take it like we would a game of chance. I said to a preacher not long ago, "Of course, we have all believed in divine healing in a certain sense." "Why," he said, "I have prayed for many people in their homes." I said "Did you expect them to get well?" "Some of them did," he said. I replied "Were you surprised when they got well?" He almost had to say yes. I said "Were you just praying and asking God, and did not know whether he would or not?" Let us come definitely about healing; let us not look at it as a game of chance and say if you are lucky you will get it and if not you will not get it.

A very honest man came to me. He was here for the first time last night. He had never before been in a revival like this. I was talking to him about healing. I said "You believe God will save all who come?" "Yes." "Why not the same with healing?" He said "Can everybody be healed?" He could not think of such a thing—everybody being healed. I said "Why not? What makes you think that some can not be healed?" He had no reason for it—just because he thought it—the thought had been handed down from generation to generation that the days of miracles are over and only occasionally God demonstrates his power in the healing of the body—when in some supernatural way it was his will for that occasion. If God ever healed anybody at all to me that is an argument that he will heal anybody who comes to him. He would not be a respecter of persons. The trouble is we have been the ones who lacked faith. He said "why is it I have not been healed?" I said "Because you have no faith." "Well," he said, "I have prayed for a long time." I said "You have prayed and at the same time you were praying you little expected to receive it." I told him of the woman who tested out Mark 11. "Say to this mountain be thou removed, plucked up, cast into the sea; and shall not doubt in his heart, but shall believe that those things which he saith shall come to pass; he shall have whatsoever he saith." There was a hill in the back yard. She said "take this hill away and be gone." The next morning the old hill was still out there. She said, "That is just like I expected." Some people hear that divine healing is so and so they try it. Some get disappointed and say "I rather thought it was not for everybody." Friends, if you do not receive healing it is your own fault, not God's fault. God wants to heal you. John said "I would that you prosper and be in health, even as your soul prospereth." Many, today are just as well physically as they are spiritually. Some people if they were as well physically as they are spiritually would be consumptives all the time. Many are about dead spiritually.

Get the Heart Right First

If you want the outward man healed, get the inward man healed. "If the spirit of Him that raised Jesus from the dead dwell in you he shall also quicken your mortal body." It is the Spirit that is to dwell in us that we want to get in our heart and life.

One reason that some people miss divine healing is because the spiritual ebb of their soul is so low there is nothing with which God can work. The Spirit of God is absolutely foreign to many professing Christians today. I do not mean Christians, I mean church members, people who make some profession of the Spirit of God but really have lost sight of the Spirit of God.

One man said it made very little difference to him whether or not Jesus was the only begotten Son of God or whether he was the Son of God at all. It made little difference in regard to Job whether there was actually a man by the name of Job or whether it was a parable. This Bible is either so or not so.

It can either be depended on or not be depended on. Christ was either the Son of God or else a fake and impostor. I believe Jesus Christ was real and I believe the Bible is real, and I believe the world needs a demonstration on the part of the Christian people of practicing the reality there is in the Bible.

A Demonstration Needed

They went to Charles Finney and wanted to know of him whether he would like them to pray for him. He said no. They asked why? He said, "You don't get your prayers answered anyway, why should you pray for me?" When the world can see us getting answers to prayer it will believe in our God. When Elijah demonstrated that God was alive and that God answered by fire, the people served Elijah's God. The gods of Baal could not answer by fire. Elijah made fun of them, and he told them to cry a little louder. He said the God who answers by fire let him be God. We ought to have a God who answers by fire today if we want people to believe there is a real God.

The Bible has not changed. It is just as real as it ever was. We as Christians should step forward and believe God's Word as he said it.

Do we have to ask God if it is his will? God says that they shall lay their hands on the sick and they shall recover. Does that mean if they get better right away they will recover? No. Supposing I say, "To-morrow I will give you $10." You went out of the door and bruise your nose and break a couple of limbs. Does that change the fact that I said that tomorrow I will give you ten dollars? No. If God says in his Word they shall lay their hands on the sick and they shall recover, if you feel well or do not feel well does that change God's Word in the least? No. Believing God and taking him at his Word is believing in spite of any other evidence. Noah was 120 years in building the ark when there was no sign of a flood at all. God said there would be a flood. If God says "they shall lay their hands on the sick and they shall recover" why can not we say they shall lay their hands on the sick and they shall recover? Why can not we repeat it and believe it without any hesitancy? Why should we be afraid to say anything the Bible says? I am not a bit more afraid to preach salvation for the body than I am for the soul. God heals both of them. It was when I first began to think of it. I said, "What will happen if I preach it and nobody gets healed?" I found out when I preached it, it was not a case of whether they got healed. They do get healed if you preach it.

When I first started out one verse came to me— that they who put their trust in him shall never be confounded. I had some awful onslaughts from the devil and it looked like he would sweep everything in sight, but God held the battle up and we came out all right. We do not have to qualify what is in the Bible. We are not responsible for it—only to preach the Word. If you are sick tonight God wants to heal you if you will just let him do it. Just believe he will do it. Why not believe him for a perfect and complete healing instead of a partial healing? Christ wants to meet all your needs.